Husserl and Frege

Studies in Phenomenology and Existential Philosophy

Husserl and Frege

J. N. Mohanty

Indiana University Press *Bloomington*

Manufactured in the United States of America

Library of Congress Cataloging in Publication Data

Mohanty, Jitendranath, 1928–
   Husserl and Frege.

   (Studies in phenomenology and existential philosophy)
   Includes bibliographical references and index.
   1. Husserl, Edmund, 1859–1938—Addresses, essays,
lectures. 2. Frege, Gottlob, 1848–1925—Addresses,
essays, lectures. 3. Phenomenology—Addresses, essays,
lectures. 4. Analysis (Philosophy)—Addresses, essays,
lectures. I. Title. II. Series.
B3279.H94M563   193   81–48554
ISBN 0–253–32878–0   AACR2
1 2 3 4 5 86 85 84 83 82

CONTENTS

PREFACE

This essay is partly historical and partly philosophical in its orientation. Chapters 1 and 2 are more historical, chapters 3 and 4 are more philosophical. None is merely one or the other. Although my research on this theme began with the purpose of reconstructing a more accurate picture of the historical situation than was then available, in the present essay I have also tried to throw some light on the issues and problems with which the two philosophers, Husserl and Frege, were concerned. Since two major components of contemporary philosophy—phenomenology and analytic philosophy—are usually traced back to these two men, it is hoped that this essay will facilitate an understanding between those two components. In my view, the differences between them have been exaggerated. This study, I hope, will show that phenomenology and analytic philosophy started with common problems and concerns, and that there are distinct conceptual routes leading from one to the other. It also aims at suggesting how the philosophical insights derived from both can be fruitfully integrated to yield a rich theory of meaning and mental life.

In chapter 1, I make use of an earlier paper from the year 1973. Parts of chapter 3 were read at a Summer Institute on Phenomenology in Berkeley, California, during the summer of 1980. Large parts of the manuscript were discussed in a weekly study group that met in Norman, Oklahoma, during the fall semester of 1980. Parts of it were also presented in Calcutta during the summer of 1981. To all those who participated in the discussions, in Berkeley, Norman, and Calcutta, I am grateful: especially to Hubert Dreyfus and Dagfinn Føllesdal; but also to John Biro, Frank Kirkland, Charlie Brown, and Katharine Mulford. Ms. Claire Hill made available to me her Paris thesis on Husserl and Frege, and thereby put me under obligation: her thesis succeeded in drawing attention to many overlooked aspects of the subject matter. Many friends have encouraged me to write this book: of these, I must specially mention Jim Edie and Elizabeth Ströker. I also thank Dr. Robert W. Shahan, editor of the *Southwestern Journal of Philosophy*, for permission to reprint the Frege-Husserl correspondence as an appendix to this book. It originally appeared in *Southwestern Journal of Philosophy*, V, 1974.

Aron Gurwitsch expressed considerable interest in my early results. This book is dedicated to his memory.

J. N. Mohanty

Husserl and Frege

CHAPTER 1

Historical Considerations

Edmund Husserl's first work, *Philosophie der Arithmetik*,[1] was published in 1891. Gottlob Frege wrote a highly critical, often sarcastic, review of this book in 1894.[2] Husserl's *Prolegomena to a Pure Logic*, the first volume of the *Logical Investigations*, appeared in 1900.[3] In the *Prolegomena*, Husserl tried systematically to refute psychologism as a theory of logic and formulated a concept of pure logic, that contrasts sharply with the psychologism Frege had found him guilty of in the *Philosophie der Arithmetik*. In the Foreword to the second edition of the *Prolegomena*, Husserl writes that the work is essentially a reworking of lectures he gave at Halle during the year 1896.[4] In his careful and pioneering study of the relation between Frege and Husserl during these years, Dagfin Føllesdal asks the question, at what point of time between 1891 (the year of publication of *Philosophie der Arithmetik*) and 1896 (the year of Halle lectures) did this change in Husserl's mode of thinking take place?[5] The papers published during 1891–93 do not, according to Føllesdal, bear testimony to any such change. In the paper "Psychologische Studien zur Elementaren Logik" of 1894, Husserl is still found to believe that the foundations of logic can be clarified with the help of psychology. Accordingly, the change must have occurred between the years 1894 and 1896. Frege's famed review of the *Philosophie der Arithmetik* appeared in 1894. Føllesdal therefore conjectures that it is Frege's review which must have led Husserl to a complete revision of his prior mode of thinking.[6] This view about the Frege-Husserl relationship is shared by many writers. A recent writer even speaks of Husserl's "traumatic encounter with Frege."[7]

In this chapter I wish to argue that the basic change in Husserl's mode of thinking which by itself could have led to the *Prolegomena* conception of pure logic had already taken place by 1891. This change may be discerned in Husserl's review of Schröder's *Vorlesungen über die Algebra der Logik*.[8] It also underlies the program of *Inhaltslogik* worked out in "Der Folgerungskalkül und die Inhaltslogik" of the same year.[9] If pure logic is defined in the *Prolegomena* in terms of the concept of ideal objective meanings,[10] then the 1891 review of Schröder's work already contains this concept. If the major burden of Frege's 1894 review of the *Philosophie der Arithmetik* is the lack of distinction, in that work, between the subjective and the objective,[11] between *Vorstellung* and *Begriff* and between both and the object, then Husserl already had come to distinguish between *Vorstellung*, meaning, and object in his 1891 review. If this be so, then another historical judgment—connected with the above—needs to be revised. It has been held by many that Husserl's distinction, in the *Logische Untersuchungen*, between meaning and object of an expression is Fregean in origin. Thus, for example, Hubert Dreyfus writes: "Husserl simply accepted and applied Frege's distinctions. . . . The only change Husserl made in Frege's analysis was terminological."[12] Now, if Husserl's review of Schröder already contains that distinction, then it surely antedates the publication of Frege's celebrated paper "Über Sinn und Bedeutung" of 1892, and Husserl must have arrived at it independently of Frege.

Referring to Schröder's distinction between univocal and equivocal names, Husserl writes:

> he lacks the true concept of the meaning of a name. That requirement of univocity is also expressed in the form: "The name shall be of a . . . constant meaning." (48) However, according to the relevant discussions on pages 47–48, the author identifies the meaning of the name with the presentation (*Vorstellung*) of the object named by the name, from which the striking consequence follows, to be sure, that all common names are equivocal. It is not as if the author had overlooked the distinction between equivocal and common names—and besides, who could overlook it! But to see a distinction and to apprehend its essence are two different things. Moreover, he uses the term "meaning" (*Bedeutung*) itself equivocally, and that in an already intolerable degree. In the above quotation, in spite of mutually op-

posed and false explanations, what is intended is the ordinary sense. On another occasion, however, what is actually meant is the object named by the name; how otherwise, e.g., could, in verbal contradiction with the above mentioned requirement, the common names be as such characterized as being such that "several meanings are true of them with the same right and justification"! (69) And even that is not enough; the class corresponding to the common name is also called its meaning (69fn.). It is therefore understandable that the author is not able to formulate the essence of equivocation precisely. . . . It is further connected with unclarity in the concept of meaning that Schröder regards names such as "round square" as meaningless (unsinnige) and sets them apart from univocal and equivocal names. Obviously he confuses here between two different questions: (1) whether there belongs to a name a meaning (ein "Sinn"); and (2) whether an object corresponding to a name exists or not.[13]

This paragraph clearly shows that Husserl did distinguish, as early as 1891, between:

(1) the sense or meaning of a term (for which he is using both 'Bedeutung' and 'Sinn', though in the Logische Untersuchungen he will prefer 'Bedeutung'),
(2) the object (Gegenstand) which the name may designate in case the object exists, and
(3) the presentation (Vorstellung) of such an object.

Presentations may vary, but the meaning or Sinn may remain the same. Further, there may be no object that is designated, and yet a name may have meaning. Even when there are objects that are designated, the multiplicity of objects does not imply multiplicity of meanings. He therefore has a clear distinction between Vorstellung, Gegenstand, and Bedeutung or Sinn.

It is true that these remarks do not contain the thesis of the ideal objectivity of meanings, but they certainly do not confuse meaning with Vorstellung and therefore testify to an awareness of the objectivity of meanings as contrasted with the subjectivity of the Vorstellungen.

Could Husserl have derived this threefold distinction from any of Frege's earlier writings? If anywhere in Frege's writings before 1891, we should look for it in Die Grundlagen der Arithmetik (1884). But Frege writes in his letter to Husserl of 24 May 1891 that he had not yet in the Grundlagen drawn the distinction between meaning and reference.[14] It is unlikely, then, that Husserl took it

from him. It is more likely that both arrived at the distinction independently, as Husserl writes back to Frege: "I also notice, that in
spite of essential points of divergence, our points of view have
many things in common. Many observations which forced themselves on me, I find had been expressed by you many years earlier."
That seems in principle to be a true account of their relationship at
this stage, though it would seem that on this point, the distinction
between meaning and reference, Husserl and Frege must have arrived at it about the same time and independently of each other.

What is of importance for our present purpose, however, is that
Husserl's overcoming of subjectivism in favor of an objective
theory of meaning and the consequent theory of logic is already
foreshadowed in the 1891 review of Schröder's work and three
years prior to Frege's review of the *Philosophie der Arithmetik*.
The other 1891 paper, the one on *Inhaltslogik*, more clearly brings
this out.

II

Among the major theses which Husserl puts forward, insofar as
his conception of logic at this point is concerned, we may mention
the following:

(1) A calculus qua calculus is not a language: "the two concepts
are fundamentally different. Language is not a method of
systematic-symbolic inference, calculus is not a method of
systematic-symbolic expression of psychic phenomena."[15]

(2) A logic qua logic is not a calculus. A calculus is a technic, a
Zeichentechnik. Logic is concerned, not with mere signs, but with
conceptual contents.[16]

(3) Deductive logic is not the same as a technic of inference, nor
is it exhausted by a theory of inference. There are deductive operations other than inferring. A deductive science does not consist
only in inferences. It may involve, e.g., the operation 'computing'
(*Rechnen*) which is not inferring.[17]

(4) It is not true that only an extensional calculus of classes is
possible. A calculus of conceptual contents, or intensions, is also
possible.[18]

(5) An autonomous extensional logic of classes is not possible,
for every extensional judgment (*Umfangsurteil*) is, in truth, an intensional judgment (*Inhaltsurteil*). The concept of class

presupposes the concepts of 'conceptual content' and 'object of a concept.'[19]

(6) Every judgment has two aspects: logical content and 'algorithmic content'.[20] The logical content is the judged content (*Urteilsgehalt*)—that which it states (*das, was sie behauptet*). When a categorical judgment is reduced to relation of subsumption among classes, this brings out its algorithmic content. The two are equivalent, but not always identical. They are identical when the judgment is a judgment about classes.

(7) A judgment by itself is directed not toward classes or conceptual contents, but toward objects of concepts (*Begriffs-gegenstände*).[21]

(8) Geometrical thinking is not operation with signs or figures. The signs are mere 'supports' for the conception of the truly intended operations with concepts and with respective objects of those concepts.[22]

Most of these theses are retained, with modifications and shifts in emphasis no doubt, in the *Prolegomena* and the *Investigations*. Pure logic is the science of meanings. "Everything that is logical falls under the two correlated categories of meaning and object."[23] Algorithmic methods spare us genuine deductive mental work by "artificially arranged mechanical operations on sensible signs"[24] and "their sense and justification depend on validatory thought."[25] Certainly Husserl has now, in the *Prolegomena*, much more sympathetic understanding of the "mathematicising theories of logic," and he has come to regard the mathematical form of treatment as the only scientific one which alone offers us "systematic closure and completeness."[26] But he is still cautioning us that "the mathematician is not really the pure theoretician, but only the ingenious technician, the constructor, as it were, who, looking merely to formal interconnections, builds up his theory like a technical work of art."[27] But this note of warning is mitigated by the assurance that what makes science possible is not essential insight but "scientific instinct and method,"[28] and that philosophical investigation should not meddle in the work of the specialist but should seek to "achieve insight in regard to the sense and essence of his achievements as regards method and manner."[29] The thesis that extension of a concept presupposes its intension is developed in the Second Investigation, though there is more explicit emphasis on the ideal objectivity of meanings and there is the talk of the *Inhalt* as a species.

III

Husserl sent copies of his 1891 papers to Frege. We know of this from the correspondence between the two men (see Appendix). It is worthwhile therefore to find out what Frege's responses to the Husserl papers were. In his letter of 24 May 1891, after acknowledging receipt of Husserl's *Philosophie der Arithmetik* and the papers on Schröder and *Inhaltslogik*, Frege emphasizes that the two have many ideas in common, and renews his decision to put in writing his own thoughts on Schröder's book.[30] He agrees with some of Husserl's criticisms of Schröder, e.g., Schröder's definitions of 'o' '1', 'a + b', and 'a − b'. Referring to the *Philosophie der Arithmetik*, Frege hopes that sometime in the future, time permitting, he may reply to Husserl's criticisms of his own theory of number. He draws attention to one major difference between them, and that concerns how a common name relates to its objects. Frege illustrates his own view with the help of the following scheme:

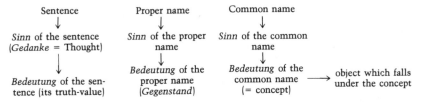

In the case of common names, one step more is needed—according to Frege—to reach the object than in the case of proper names. Further, in the case of common names, the concept may be empty: there may be no object without its ceasing thereby to be scientifically useful. In the case of proper names, however, if a name does not name anything, if it lacks an object, it is scientifically useless. This refers to Frege's well-known and controversial thesis that concepts constitute the reference, not the *Sinn*, of common names. Frege contrasts with this Husserl's view that the *Sinn* (or, in Husserl's language, the *Bedeutung*) of a common name is the concept expressed by it and its reference is constituted by the object or objects falling under the concept. The letter makes it clear that Frege does recognize that Husserl had the distinction between *Sinn* and *Gegenstand*, only here he does not ascribe to Husserl a distinction between *Vorstellung* and *Sinn*.

Husserl writes back to Frege on 18 July 1891. He admits he has derived great stimulation from Frege's theories, and goes on to express his views about the many points of agreement between them, to which reference has been made earlier. Among these points of agreement, Husserl refers to his own distinction between 'language' (*Sprache*) and 'calculus' which he now finds in Frege's 1883 paper "Über den Zweck der Begriffsschrift,"[31] where Frege distinguishes between the concept of "calculus ratiocinator" and the concept of "lingua characteristica." It appears to him that the *Begriffsschrift* is intended to be a lingua characteristica and not a "sign language constructed in imitation of the arithmetical." He concludes the letter by expressing agreement with Frege's rejection of "formal arithmetic" as a theory of arithmetic, however important it may be as an extension of the arithmetical technic. Husserl is referring to Frege's "Über formale Theorien der Arithmetik"[32] a copy of which Frege had just sent him. The sense of 'formalism' in which Frege rejects it as a theory of arithmetic is that according to which the signs for numbers like '1/2', '2/3', 'π' are empty, meaningless signs (*leere Zeichen*). According to this theory, as Frege understands it, these empty signs themselves are numbers that constitute the proper subject matter of arithmetic.[33] That Husserl should concur fully with Frege's total rejection of such a theory of arithmetic should be obvious from the foregoing summary of his views. The *Prolegomena*, however, shows much greater understanding of the significance of formalism, but even there his philosophy of arithmetic is not formalistic. His formal logic there is correlate of formal ontology, and in large parts of the work he is concerned not with a specific formal science but with the form of theory in general.

Clearly, the Frege-Husserl correspondence of 1891[34] surveyed above contains no indication that Frege recognized the presence of the *Vorstellung-Sinn* distinction in Husserl's Schröder review. However, as we have already seen, this distinction is there, and it suggests that Husserl was already on his way, independently of Frege's 1894 review, toward the objective conception of logic of the *Prolegomena*.

IV

Let us now look at other comments by Frege on the Husserl papers of 1891. We know that in his 24 May 1891 letter to Husserl, Frege writes that Husserl's Schröder review had made him decide to publish his own thoughts on Schröder's book, and that his comments on it may appear in the *Zeitschrift für Philosophie und philosophische Kritik*. However, Frege's "Kritische Beleuchtung einiger Punkte in E. Schröders Vorlesungen über die Algebra der Logik" finally appeared four years later in the *Archiv für systematische Philosophie*.[35] In this review, Frege among other things distinguishes between Schröder's concept of '*Gebiet*' (domain) and the logical concept of class, and points out how Schröder unknowingly oscillates between the two. Insofar as the logical concept of class is concerned, Frege considers it entirely mistaken to take a class as consisting in individual things, as a collection of individuals—a mistake which, according to him, derives from Schröder's attempt to extend his *Gebietekalkül* to the logic of classes.[36] And yet, asks Frege, how else is a class constituted if one abstracts from common properties? "Only through the fact that the classes are determined by the properties which their individuals should have, only through the fact that one uses expressions such as 'the class of objects which are b', is it possible to express general thoughts when one states relations amongst classes; only through this that one comes to logic."[37] Thus Frege agrees with Husserl's comments: the extension of a concept presupposes the intension of the concept. In Frege's own words: "In reality I hold the view that the concept logically precedes its extension, and I consider it a mistake to attempt to found the class, as extension of a concept, not on the concept itself but on the individual things."[38] However, despite this agreement with Husserl's point of view, Frege refuses to side with *Inhaltslogik* as against the so-called *Umfangslogik*, and adds: "Nevertheless, I am in many respects possibly closer to the author [Schröder] than to those whom one could call, in opposition to him, logicians of content (*Inhalt*)."[39] He obviously has Husserl in mind. The question naturally arises: why does Frege reject the conception of an *Inhaltslogik* even though he does not agree with a purely extensional analysis of classes?

The reasons become partly clear when one considers his remarks on *Inhaltslogik* in the essay "Ausführungen über Sinn und Bedeutung"[40] which possibly belongs to the period 1892–95. Frege writes:

> Even if one has to concede to the *Inhalts*-logicians that the concept itself, as contrasted with its extension, is the foundational, nevertheless it should not for that reason be understood as the meaning (*Sinn*) of the concept-word, but as its reference, and the *Umfangs*-logicians are nearer the truth insofar as they locate in the extension (*Umfang*) an essential meaning (*Bedeutung*) which, though not itself the concept, is yet very closely connected with it.[41]

We have already found that the *Inhaltslogik* is a logic of meanings. Although Frege regards the concept as primary and extension as derivative, he also considers the concept itself to be the reference of a concept-word. A logic of concepts, then, would be a logic not of *Sinn* but of *Bedeutungen* (in Frege's senses of those words) and hence closer to an extensional logic. The following paragraph further clarifies Frege's argument:

> They [the *Umfangs*-logicians] are right when, because of their preference for the extension of a concept to its intension, they admit that they regard the reference of words, and not their meaning, to be essential for logic. The *Inhalts*-logicians only remain too happily with the meaning, for what they call "*Inhalt*," if it is not quite the same as *Vorstellung*, is certainly the meaning (*Sinn*). They do not consider the fact that in logic it is not a question of how thoughts come from thoughts without regard to truth-value, that, more generally speaking, the progress from meanings (*Sinne*) to reference (*Bedeutung*), must be made; that the logical laws are first laws in the realm of references and only then mediately relate to meaning (*Sinn*).[42]

Also in the same essay, Frege makes reference to Husserl's distinction between whether a name has a *Sinn* and whether an object corresponding to it exists or not. But he finds this distinction insufficient, for Husserl does not distinguish between proper names and concept-words and as we saw earlier Frege differs widely from Husserl on this point. Again there is no reference to Husserl's distinction between *Vorstellung* and *Sinn*. The one likely recognition of this is the covert statement that the *Inhalt* of the *Inhalts*-logicians, if it is not *Vorstellung*, must be the *Sinn*.[43]

V

We may sum up our conclusions insofar as the Frege-Husserl relationship about the years 1891–94 is concerned:

1. The two men arrived at the *Vorstellung-Sinn* reference distinction independently of each other.

2. Husserl's overcoming of psychologism and acceptance of a theory of objective, pure logic was fundamentally independent of Frege's 1894 review of the *Philosophie der Arithmetik*. The basic change had occurred in 1891. That this should have occurred in the very year of publication of the *Philosophie der Arithmetik* is made all the more plausible by the following note by Husserl, belonging to a much later date:

> Ich las viel in der "Philosophie der Arithmetik." Wie unreif, wie naiv und fast kindlich erschien mir dieses Werk. Nun, nicht umsonst peinigte mich bei der Publikation das Gewissen. Eigentlich war ich darüber schon hinaus, als ich es publizierte. Es stammte ja im wesentlichen aus den Jahren 86/87.[44]

3. (a) Frege agrees with Husserl that the concept of a class presupposes the concept of concept, that the extension of a concept presupposes the intension.

(b) Nevertheless, while Husserl went on to develop the idea of an *Inhaltslogik* and subsequently a logic of meanings (though he did not quite reject *Umfangslogik*, to be sure, but wavered between [i] asserting a bare equivalence between the two logics and [ii] asserting the primacy of the *Inhaltslogik*), Frege sides with *Umfangslogik* for two reasons: his belief that logic is concerned not with mere consistency of thoughts but with their truth-value; and his theory that the reference of concept-words is the concept itself (as contrasted with Husserl's view, which may also be said to be the standard view, that the concept is the *Sinn* of the concept-word).[45]

VI

Further support for my conclusions is to be found in Husserl's other writings from that period, only recently published. I will focus on three essays: "Zur Logik des Zeichen" (1890),[46] "Intentionale Gegenstände" (1894)[47] and a review (1896) of Twardowski's "Zur Lehre von Inhalt."[48]

In the essay on the logic of signs, Husserl distinguishes between external signs and conceptual signs. An external sign denotes, but does not characterize. A proper name is said to be an external sign. The conceptual sign denotes through the mediation of some specific concept of the denoted. Again, a proper name is said to be a direct sign, a general name is said to be an indirect name because it denotes through mediation of conceptual marks. In the case of direct signs, we are told, that which the sign means and that which it denotes are identical; with indirect signs this is not the case.

Two signs are identical if they refer to the same object in the same manner. They are equivalent insofar as they refer to the same object but in different ways (e.g., '2 + 3' and '7 − 2').

Two other distinctions are of interest in the context of our present concern. First, names are defined as representing *matter* or *absolute contents*. Contrasted with names are form-expressions which denote relations; these expressions need supplementation, they are *ergänzungsbedürftig*. Secondly, following Brentano, judgment is defined as recognition (*Anerkennung*) of a content. Husserl writes that special signs for recognition or rejection of contents are not necessary for formal procedure. This obviously refers to Frege's assertion sign. It is surprising that the allegedly psychological logicians would have no use for such a sign, whereas the anti-psychologistic logician would find a place for it.

Also to be noted is that whereas Frege was about to develop a sense-reference distinction with regard to all names—to "Aristotle" as much as to "the evening star"—Husserl, in 1890, followed Mill with regard to genuine proper names. It took him a long time to overcome this position, if he ever did overcome it completely.

The essay on intentional objects begins by examining the proposition that every presentation (*Vorstellung*) relates to its object through a mental picture. Husserl rejects this alleged mental picture as a theoretical fiction. There is no such immanent object, he writes. Even if the act has a picture, he continues, it is not this picture that is intended, but rather the outer object. What is still more important (and this is an argument repeated in the *Logical Investigations*[49]), to understand an image as a picture *of* . . . is already to admit a new act. A picture becomes a picture *of* . . . by what he here calls the "Über-sich-hinausweisen" of the picture.

The essay then goes on to clarify the sense of "presentation" in the proposition "A presentation relates to, or presents, an object." In the "Psychologische Studien"[50] of the same year, he had confessed, "I think it is a good principle to avoid whenever possible using so equivocal a name as 'presentation'." The Second Logical Investigation repeats the caution: "The word 'presentation' has in any case a shifting multiplicity of sense. . . . One must, however, see whether the various meanings of the word are not mutually confusing, and whether its use in a characterization does not promote confusion and definite error rather than clarity."[51] In spite of these reminders, Husserl continues to use the term, always separating its different senses.

But the distinction that he makes in this 1894 essay that is relevant for our purpose is this. He insists that the subjective, psychological content (Gehalt) of a presentation must be kept apart from the ideal content (Inhalt, also called Ideal Gehalt) of a presentational act. The objective relatedness of a presentation is ascribed to its ideal content, not to its psychological contents. The ideal content is also called the meaning-content (Bedeutungsinhalt), which according to Husserl consists in features (Merkmale) which are predicates of the objects. The meaning (Bedeutung) is an inner moment of the presentation, whereas the extension (Umfang) is a secondary and external aspect. While particular presentations may have no psychological components in common, the ideal content constitutes what Husserl calls here an Identifizierungszusammenhang, an identification-structure, making possible an identity of objective reference. He then goes on to make these rather Fregean statements: presentations having the same meaning could exhibit objective differences, and presentations having different meanings an identity of objective reference. Note that Frege never held the first half of this thesis. Husserl repeats it in the First Logical Investigation.[52]

"Truth," Husserl goes on, has many meanings, but the original, "root" concept of truth, which all others presuppose, is that which relates to objective meaning contents of representations.

Finally, from this essay, a remark on method, anticipating a theme of the Sixth Logical Investigation:

In order to bring into clarity, what it means to say that a meaning means this or that thing, a statement relates to a state of affairs, a name names an object, and more generally, a representation presents an object, we could not do otherwise than picture to ourselves an intuition of fulfilment: we represent to ourselves an univocal statement and experience to evidence or an univocal nominal fulfilment, as when, e.g., we say 'red', and in unity with it, see red(?).

In the Sixth Logical Investigation, Husserl writes:

> I speak, e.g., of my inkpot, and my inkpot also stands before me: I see it . . . the name 'my inkpot' seems to *overlay* the perceived object, to belong *sensibly* to it. This belonging is of a peculiar kind.[53]

In his 1896 review of Twardowski's book Husserl further develops his ideas about the meaning content. Of the things he says there, two are worth mentioning. First, the immanent or psychological content (*Inhalt*) is said to be noticeable (*Bemerkbares*), whereas the meaning-content is not. Secondly, the immanent content is an individual, psychic datum, a here and now being, whereas the meaning-content is never an individual entity. The meaning-content does not reside in the presentation as a real component. It is rather said to be *functional*. "The function [of meaning] develops itself in discursive thinking, in judgmental structures, e.g., in identity judgments of the sort 'The presentations A and B mean the same'." The review makes a clear affirmation that "meaning (*Bedeutung*), concept (*Begriff*), in the widest sense, and presentation (*Vorstellung*) in the proper logical sense are synonymous."

VII

The purpose of these historical considerations has been to show that the seeds of development of Husserl's philosophy from the *Philosophie der Arithmetik* to the *Prolegomena* were immanent to his own thinking,[54] so that the hypothesis of a traumatic effect of Frege's 1894 review of his book and a consequent reversal of his mode of thinking is not only uncalled for but also unsubstantiated by available evidence. This is not to deny that both as a result of that review and as a result of a greater appreciation of the formal-deductive nature of mathematics, Husserl changed his views about Frege's strongly anti-psychologistic theory of number. In many respects, as Føllesdal so well demonstrates, Husserl's views in the *Logical Investigations* come closer to Frege's. But to recognize this is not tantamount to saying either (i) that Husserl's position in the *Philosophie der Arithmetik* was in fact precisely understood and effectively criticized by Frege or (ii) that Frege's criticism is what led to Husserl's position in the *Prolegomena*. In fact, as I will argue in the next chapter, Frege did not correctly grasp what Husserl was doing in that first work; and if Husserl was in fact guilty of psychologism, his was psychologism of a sort that is different from both what Frege criticized in the review and what Husserl himself refuted in the *Prolegomena*.

It is rather more likely that both Frege and Husserl were influenced, in their anti-psychologism and in their advocacy of a pure logic, by Lotze. Frege heard Lotze's lectures in Göttingen.[55] Husserl explicitly admits to having been influenced by Lotze. In a draft of the Foreword to the second edition of the *Logical Investigations*,[56] he recalls three sources of influence on him during the years 1886–1895. First, studies in the areas of formal mathematics and formal logic and in Leibniz, particularly his distinction between truths of fact and truths of reason (as also Hume's distinction between 'relations of ideas' and 'matters of fact'),[57] were primarily responsible for the overcoming of psychologism. Secondly, the so-called Platonism that accompanied this anti-psychologism is traced to the influence of Lotze's *logic*. Lotze's influential Plato interpretation, his talk of truths in themselves, suggested the possibility of regarding all mathematical truths and logical principles as belonging to the domain of idealities. Finally, of course, Bolzano, whose elaborate theory of presentations in themselves, propositions in themselves, and truths in themselves, first misunderstood (by Husserl himself) as metaphysical hypersubtleties, subsequently led him completely to revise his logic lectures. Both Lotze and Bolzano, in Husserl's estimation, had their serious deficiencies, but they both pointed to him the way out at a time when he was groping for it.

The only two references to Frege in the *Logical Investigations* are appreciative. One of them,[58] a footnote to an affirmation of the fundamental heterogeneity of the two sciences mathematics and psychology, refers us both to Natorp's influential paper "Über objektive und subjektive Begründung der Erkenntnis" and to Frege's *Die Grundlagen der Arithmetik* of 1884. Husserl adds that he no longer approves of the fundamental criticisms of Frege's anti-psychological position that he had made in his *Philosophie der Arithmetik*, and also refers approvingly to Frege's Preface to the *Grundgesetze*. The other[59] is intended to distinguish between his own terminology and Frege's. Although these brief references contain no indication of an acknowledgment by Husserl of his debt to Frege, they certainly show that he recognized the affinity between their positions.

VIII

For gaining the proper historical perspective which this chapter is intended to foster, it is also necessary to bear in mind that even after 1894, when Husserl did develop his strongly anti-psychologistic concept of pure logic and worked out a theory of ideality of meanings, that theory is still far from being Fregean. The ideal meanings, for Husserl's theory at this point of time, are species whose instantiations are the particular mental acts whose meanings they are. This is the thesis, in other words, that meanings are essences instantiated in mental acts; they are essential structures of those acts.[60] It was around 1906 that this form of the theory was revised in favor of a more Fregean version, for which meanings are intentional correlates of the acts, not their immanent, real, essential structure. Güdo Küng's suggestion that the revival of Husserl-Frege correspondence around 1906 had something to do with this revision is not borne out by the contents of the letters from that year; they deal with quite different issues.[61]

Nor do Frege's and Husserl's concepts of pure logic coincide. At this stage, I can recall only a few major points of difference: first of all, Frege thought of logic as a normative science,[62] whereas Husserl, in his rather extreme anti-psychologism, suspected that the normative conception may indeed be a secret ally of psychologism, and is certainly a poor defense against it. Husserl therefore thought of logic as a pure theoretical science, its normative role being derivative and founded on its theoretical principles.

Second, the most fundamental concept of logic for Frege is the concept of truth-value. For Husserl it is the concept of meaning. Even if both made a sense-reference distinction, Husserl excluded any concern with reference from pure logic. Frege did precisely the opposite. One cannot resist the surmise (made indeed by many)[63] that the point of Frege's sense-reference distinction, insofar as logic is concerned, was to exclude all considerations of sense, and to have a logic only of references, that is, of truth-values. One then understands why, although Frege clearly rejected an extensional theory of concepts (i.e., a reduction of concept to class) and in this agreed with Husserl as against Schröder, he believed logic to be extensional. For both concepts and truth values are references, not *Sinne*. It is curious that Frege should have accused the *Inhalts-*

logicians of looking for differences in *Sinne* and not for equivalence (i.e., identity in reference), when he himself believed that the *Sinne* are not subjective and private.[64]

IX

The question of the relation between Husserl and Frege, to which this chapter is devoted, is, however, more than a merely "historical" question. More important, for me, than the historical issues such as who influenced whom are the strictly philosophical issues involved. Let me conclude this "historically" oriented chapter by indicating two broad philosophical perspectives for a discussion of our theme:

In the first place, it is important to keep in mind that Husserl and Frege belonged to *nearly* the same philosophical world, in which a sort of neo-Kantian philosophy prevailed (which Husserl under Brentano's influence *tried* to overcome but never quite succeeded, but with which Frege all along had great sympathies), in which Hermann Lotze was the towering figure, in which what was labeled as "psychologism" was a widely held philosophy of logic, and in which philosophers were concerned with such concepts as mental acts, *Inhalt* or content of those acts, and made liberal use of the concept of *Vorstellung* or presentation. Within this world, neither Frege nor Husserl offered the first critique of psychologism. Both took it up anew. Both asserted the independence of logic from psychology—Frege first, Husserl subsequently. But Husserl, even after his detailed criticisms in the *Prolegomena*, again and again returned to the theme of psychologism, and continued to wonder if the concept of "psychologism" and its roots had been adequately laid bare in that early work (which shows the thinness of the charge that he again relapsed into it.) Thus, their overall philosophical concerns had many things in common. What divided them was not their answers to their common problems, but Frege's interest in a *Begriffschrift*, and Husserl's interest in the constituting role of the intentional life of consciousness. We need, however, to go back to the area of agreement that preceded this divergence.

In the second place, it is hoped that a clear understanding of the relationship between these two philosophers will in turn help us to understand the relationship between phenomenology and analytic philosophy by showing us how, starting from a common set of concerns and often from a common set of distinctions and theses, Husserl on the one hand and Frege's followers on the other could have developed in such different directions that Western philosophy was split into two groups between which there was virtually no fruitful communication.

CHAPTER 2

The Issue of Psychologism

In 1894 Frege published his review of Husserl's *Philosophie der Arithmetik*. It was not the first time he had criticized psychologism. In all the major works published prior to the review—the *Begriffsschrift* (1879), the *Grundlagen* (1884), and the *Grundgesetze* (1893)—as well as in the paper "Sinn und Bedeutung" (1892), Frege had unambiguously and vehemently rejected it.[1] The review, therefore, insofar as psychologism is concerned, contains nothing new. Since our interest now is precisely in the question of psychologism, we shall disregard Frege's points about Husserl's philosophy of arithmetic that have no direct bearing on this question, and take up only those which are relevant to it.

(1) Since for Husserl, in the *Philosophie der Arithmetik*, numbers are predicates of totalities and totalities are formed by the relation of collective combination, which is a "psychic" relation, the numbers become mental entities, presentations, results of mental processes or activities. Concepts of numbers require a further reflection on the mental acts of collective combination.

(2) Husserl holds, in *Philosophie der Arithmetik*, that in order to form a totality one must completely abstract from the particularities of the individual contents. Here, to abstract from something is the same as ignoring it altogether. Frege calls this process "cleansing in the psychological wash-tub," which makes things "absolutely the same as one another without altering them."

(3) For psychologism, everything becomes presentation. Spe-

cifically for logic, presentation and the object of which it is the presentation ('moon' and 'the presentation of the moon') are not distinguished. Like objects, concepts also become—that is, are confused with—presentations. To apply a concept to an object, on this theory, is to abstract from, i.e., not to attend to the object's irrelevant features. But by this process, the object becomes more and more insubstantial. Even after that, we still need to reflect on the mental acts involved in the entire psychological process.

(4) Not only is the object made subjective, the subjective presentation is treated as if it could be separated from the person who owns it and then observed in public. But presentations are essentially subjective and private. No two persons may have the same presentation. No one can even compare his presentation with another's in order to be able to say whether they are the same or different, for in order to be able to do so, the two presentations must be brought under one consciousness without undergoing any alterations, which just is not possible.

(5) Psychological logicians do not distinguish between *sense* and *presentation*. Consequently, unlike mathematicians, they are not satisfied with an extensional definition, but rather look for the *content* of the concept to be defined. The content could not be the sense, for "the dissected sense simply is not the original one." What, then, they are looking for is the presentation. An extensional definition is considered (wrongly) to be inadequate, if the definiendum and the definiens have different contents, i.e., presentations.

(6) The psychological logician can have no account of identity. If words designated presentations, one could never say "A is the same as B."

Besides the review, there are numerous other places where Frege returns to his favorite theme of psychologism. One important point he makes there is this: (7) Psychologism does not distinguish between "being true" and "being taken for true." The proper task of logic is to find the laws of being-true, not those of taking-to-be-true. Taking what is false for true and taking what is true for true, both alike arise in accordance with psychological laws. The latter therefore do not suffice to account for the distinction between truth and falsity, i.e., between justified taking-to-be-true and unjustified taking-to-be-true.[2]

II

In order to be able to decide the pertinence of Frege's criticisms as well as ascertain their influence on the subsequent development of Husserl's philosophy, we need to answer three questions:

(a) What is meant by "psychologism"?
(b) Is Husserl's position in the *Philosophie der Arithmetik* psychologistic?
(c) What elements of his *Philosophie der Arithmetik* thesis were clearly retracted by Husserl?

(a) What is meant by "psychologism"? Although psychologism could be proposed as a theory which makes *empirical* psychology the explanatory basis alike for logic and theory of knowledge, ethics and aesthetics, the psychologism issue as it was debated among German philosophers of the late nineteenth century concerned only logic and theory of knowledge. Erdmann, who was probably the first to use the appellation "psychologism," used it to designate the thesis that the logical principles such as the principle of non-contradiction derive their necessity from "the essence of our presentation and thinking." Erdmann was, of course, preceded by a long tradition of psychological, and even physiological, interpretation of the Kantian *a priori* — of which Fries and Helmholtz were the great champions. Psychologism, then, as it was vehemently attacked by Frege and later by Husserl, is to be understood — as Husserl tells us on a later occasion — as *logical* psychologism.[3]

Now, logical psychologism may be either weak or strong.[4] Weak logical psychologism holds the view that the essential theoretical foundations of logic lie in psychology, so that psychological inquiry into actual human thought processes constitutes necessary, but not sufficient, conditions for inquiring into the foundations of logic. Strong logical psychologism considers logic to be a branch of psychology, the laws of logic to be descriptive laws of actual human thought process, and understands those laws as making assertions about mental events — from all of which it would appear to follow that for this variety of logical psychologism, psychological inquiry into actual human thought processes constitutes both necessary and sufficient conditions for inquiry into the foundations of logic.

(b) Keeping this distinction in mind, we can say that Husserl's *Philosophy of Arithmetic* was *at most* guilty of weak logical psychologism, that he certainly never espoused logical psychologism of the strong variety.[5] What, however, Husserl most vehemently attacks in the *Prolegomena*, and what Frege attacks in his Review, is strong logical psychologism. In *Philosophie der Arithmetik*, arithmetic is not regarded as a branch of psychology, or arithmetical laws as laws of actual human thought processess; rather, the senses of the fundamental concepts of arithmetic are sought to be clarified by tracing them back to their origin in intuitive presentations, certain acts of abstraction and combination, and reflection on those acts. The theory does not claim to provide a foundation for logic in the same sense as Hilbert's formalism or Frege's logicism. Its claim and purpose is to *clarify* the fundamental concepts in a sense of 'clarification' that is never fully abandoned by Husserl.

If by 'psychologism' is meant the thesis that the object of an act is identical with the act (sound heard = hearing of the sound, sense-datum = sensation), Husserl rejects it from the beginning.[6] Indeed, his affiliation to the Brentano school rules out the possibility of his ever having had held this view. On the other hand, if it is the view that the content (*Inhalt*) is immanent in the act, Husserl never rejects it in part, especially insofar as the 'primary contents' or matter are concerned. However, such immanent contents were never for Husserl the intended object.

The charge of strong psychologism which Frege levels against the *Philosophie der Arithmetik*, then, rests upon the thesis that totalities are made possible by collective combination, and that formal categories, such as numbers, originate in the act of reflection upon appropriate acts. Now, as regards the concept of collective combination, it has been recently argued by Dallas Willard that Husserl *calls* it a "psychic relation" only because, and in the sense that, its manner of forming objects into a whole, such that the nature of their particular contents makes no difference at all, is phenomenally similar to the manner in which the act-object relation includes objects into a whole. The total variability of the terms combined, and the fact that the relation itself, unlike in the case of the so-called physical relations, cannot be found among the things related, make it so much like the act-object relation that it is called "psychic," although of all so-called psychic relations only the act-object relation is a mental or subjective relation in the strict sense. It is probable that Husserl's terminology here, and possibly an aspect of the substantive thesis, was due to the influence of Brentano's view that if something is not 'physical', it has to be called 'psychical', and that the so-called ideal entities are fictions.[7] Husserl, under the influence of Brentano, might later have thought of this thesis as an instance of psychologism, but it is interesting to note what he has to say about it as late as 1913. In the draft of a preface to the second edition of the *Logical Investigations*,[8] he writes that there certainly was something right in the thesis that the presentation of the totality arises out of collective combination. But since the collection is not a contentual unity grounded in the contents of the combined terms, it appears to him—in accordance with the preconception that everything intuitively apprehended must be either "physical" or "psychical"—that since the collection could not be physical, it had to be *psychic*; that is, the concept of collection had to originate through psychological reflection on the act of collecting (as much as the concept of unity arose through reflection on the act of positing something). It is important to note that the two theses are independent of each other, and that only the second one entails some sort of psychologism. A totality is different from the *concept* of collection: the former arises through collective combination, the latter through reflection on the act of combining. Since collective combinations' being called "psychic," as said earlier, does not amount to making the totality subjective, this thesis by itself is not psychologism. However, if the concepts of totalities, which are numbers, arise through reflection upon the acts of combination, we run the risk of psychologism. In the 1913 draft of a preface, Husserl writes that the concept of number is essentially different from the concept of combining. It is the latter concept, but not the former, which arises through reflection upon appropriate acts.

(c) We thus find that Frege's review attacks, in the main, a variety of psychologism which was not Husserl's in the *Philosophie der Arithmetik*. This is not to imply that many of Frege's criticisms of Husserl's theory of number are not pertinent. But Frege is wrong in ascribing to Husserl a strong psychologism and his criticisms of such a psychologism, in themselves valid, are wide of the mark insofar as Husserl's project, and execution of that project, in the *Philosophie der Arithmetik* are concerned. After Husserl eventually published his own critique of psychologism, which of the theses of the *Philosophie der Arithmetik* did he explicitly take back or drastically modify?

(1) That some account of the mental processes by which fundamental concepts of logic acquire their *clarified* sense is necessary for a grounding of logic, remains an abiding ingredient of Husserl's thinking. As the precise sense of this account, and of "clarification," becomes clearer, the idea of a phenomenological grounding of logic also becomes clearer. Although by 1897 Husserl has overcome whatever psychologism there was in the *Philosophie der Arithmetik*, he is still writing in that year that the descriptive and genetic investigation of the phenomena of intuition, representation, and apperception are necessary for founding every theory of judgment.[9]

In the *Selbstanzeige* of the *Prolegomena*, published in the same year as the book itself,[10] Husserl, after stating his conception of pure logic, writes: "An *adequate* clarification of pure logic, that is, a clarification of its essential concepts and theories, its relation to all other sciences and of the manner it determines them, requires very deep phenomenological (i.e., pure descriptive, not genetic-psychological) and epistemological investigations." He has now set aside *genetic* psychology. Phenomenology is still descriptive and eidetic psychology.

(2) The *Philosophie der Arithmetik*, as we have seen, requires three kinds of acts for the constitution of concept of number (as also for all categorial concepts): first the act of abstraction by which even the most diverse objects are reduced to *somethings*, then the act of collective combination which generates the totality [something, something, something, . . .], and, finally, the act of reflection on the first two acts, which is supposed to yield the concept of number. Of these three sorts of acts, Husserl clearly rejects the role of the last, and greatly revises his account of the first.

The concept of number or even of a totality is not derived from reflection on the acts of combination. As Findlay puts it, "mental doings may help to make them possible, may help to 'constitute' their sense or their objects, as the mature doctrine of Husserl abundantly recognizes, but they plainly form no part of their 'content'."[11] Husserl does not merely recognize this in the aforementioned preface. He makes the same point in §44 of the Sixth Logical Investigation more systematically and in a broader context, i.e., with regard to all logical-ontological categories.

"It is a natural but quite misguided doctrine," he writes, "universally put about since the time of Locke, that the meanings in question (or the corresponding substantively hypostatized meanings)—the *logical categories* such as being and non-being, unity, plurality, totality, number, ground, consequence, etc.—arise through *reflection upon certain mental acts, and so fall in the sphere of 'inner sense', of 'inner perception'.*"[12] This view is correct, he continues, with regard to such concepts as perception, judging, affirmation, denial, collecting, counting, etc., but not with regard to the first group of concepts which "cannot at all be regarded as concepts of mental acts, or of then real constituents." With regard to aggregates, the new thesis, then, amounts to this:

> An aggregate, e.g., is given, and can only be given, in an actual act of assembly, in an act, that is, expressed in the conjunctive form of connection A *and* B *and* C . . . But the concept of *Aggregate* does not arise through reflection on this act: instead of paying heed to the act which presents an aggregate, we have rather to pay heed to what it presents, to the *aggregate* it renders apparent in *concreto*, and then to lift the universal form of our aggregate to conceptually universal consciousness.[13]

An equally drastic change takes place in the concept of abstraction. In *Philosophie der Arithmetik*, Husserl subscribed to the theory of abstraction as a function of attention. In the Second Logical Investigation, as is well known, this theory is severely criticized as one of the nominalistic theories of abstraction whose main error, we are told, lies "in quite ignoring the irreducible peculiarities of the forms of consciousness (of the forms of our intentions and of their correlative fulfilments)."[14] The formal categories such as "something" are rather constituted by the process of "formalization" which is an act *sui generis*.[15]

In spite of these changes in his viewpoint, Husserl still holds on to an important part of the *Philosophie der Arithmetik* thesis about collective combinations. Collective combination, we were then told, is a relation which cannot be found out by merely considering the contents of the things related, it does not belong among the contents of the presentation. This much of the thesis is still retained in the *Logical Investigations*: the objective correlates of *categorial* forms, he writes, are *not real* moments of the contents that enter into those forms.[16] 'Real', in this new formulation, is defined as "object of possible sense-perception." The thesis now amounts to this, that the logical-ontological elements of our thoughts (components such as 'a', 'the', 'and', 'or', 'if') find their fulfilling confirmation not in sense-perception but in what Husserl comes to call categorial intuition.

3. As a result of these changes, and also because of much greater clarity regarding the act-content-object distinction (which, Husserl writes in 1913, he already had made while writing *Philosophie der Arithmetik*, but "wusste doch nichts damit anzufangen"[17]), he comes to realize that his own criticisms in *Philosophie der Arithmetik* of Frege's anti-psychologistic position were not acceptable to him any longer. Husserl had raised several objections to Frege's concept of number.[18] Some of these, I think, were *not* covered by this confession. In particular, two of his criticisms would still be acceptable to him. One is that Frege's definition of "the number attaching to a concept F" as the extension of the concept "having the same number as the concept F" does not define the content of the concept of the number, but only its extension. Frege considers this intensionalism to be a consequence of psychologism. This indeed is strange, for Frege would be the last to regard the meaning or sense, which is what the intensionalist wants to define, as a psychological entity. Frege's more persuasive reply is that the extensional definition serves all the purposes of mathematics. This is fine, but does not justify the claim that a definition need not consider the sense at all. Church rightly rejects Frege's answer on the ground that this would reduce the theorem "Every equilateral triangle is equiangular" to triviality.[19] Secondly, Husserl argues that a number attaches, not to a concept as Frege would have it, but to an extension, i.e., a collection of entities. Of a concept, Husserl admits, one may predicate the property of having a certain number only indirectly. Now, Church has pointed out that the two notions "number of a concept" and "number of an extension" are definable in terms of each other. We may therefore choose either of the two. This, in fact, is in accordance with Husserl's position in an 1891 paper, "Der Folgerungskalkül und die Inhaltslogik." Strictly speaking, in *Philosophie der Arithmetik*, the concepts such as 'unity', 'plurality', and 'number' are indefinables.

We are now in a position to surmise the effect of Frege's review on Husserl. That the review impressed him a great deal in undoubtedly true. Boyce Gibson recalls Husserl telling him that "Frege's criticism was the only one he was really grateful for. It hit the nail on the head."[20] However, this does not support the view that the review led Husserl to abandon his psychologism and led him to his conception of pure logic. It did lead him to revise some parts of his theory of number, it must have made him perceive the need of a careful terminology[21] for distinguishing between act, content, and object, and certainly must have impressed upon him the ruinous consequences of a variety of psychologism which he himself never subscribed to.

III

We are now in a position to compare Husserl's and Frege's attitudes toward psychologism, psychology, and the subjective in general.

(a) Føllesdal has noted that whereas Frege did not think it possible to refute psychologism by adducing "objectively valid arguments" against it, Husserl claimed, in the *Prolegomena*, precisely to be doing so.[22] The reason for this difference is not hard to see. Føllesdal argues that since, according to Frege, the truth of a logical law can only be demonstrated with the help of another logical law, and since this procedure must come to a stop, there is a limit to a logical demonstration of the truths of logic. Husserl, however, could claim to refute psychologism logically and thereby to give a logical demonstration of the objective validity of logical principles, because the appeal to *Evidenz* is a necessary part of his objectively valid proof. An appeal to "evidence," for Frege, is a concealed psychologism. A confession that psychologism cannot be conclusively refuted by objectively valid arguments would be, for Husserl, a final surrender to relativism, an anticlimax for Frege's lifelong battle against psychologism.

In the context of this situation of the problem, it is of interest to find a revival of this discussion in a current philosophical journal. In his paper "Psychologism in Logic: Husserl's Critique,"[23] Jack Meiland begins with the question whether other laws of logic than we now have are conceivable. Philosophers who hold the view that the laws of logic are conventions must reply that other laws of logic are indeed possible, but then they have to tell us what criterion of possibility they are using other than that which follows from the logical laws we have at our disposal. The anticonventionalist who holds that the laws of logic describe the necessary structure of reality must give a satisfactory explanation of *why* this structure is necessary, why any other structure is inconceivable. Psychologism, as a theory of logic, helps us at this point, according to Meiland: it explains why our laws of logic seem necessary to us, and why alternative laws are inconceivable, not in terms of reality, or in terms of conventions, but in terms of the structure of our minds. Meiland defends such a psychologism against Husserl's objections. Although, as Husserl insists, one can deny the law of non-contradiction even if that law were a law of our mind, for Meiland, denying the law is nothing more than *saying* 'The law of non-contradiction is false' and does not amount to genuine thought in the sense of understanding what one is saying. Second, Husserl's point that on the psychologistic theory logical truths would be contingently necessary (necessary, for they follow from logical laws, and contingent, for those laws themselves are contingent) has no great merit, because the idea of contingent necessity makes perfectly good sense. Third, Husserl misconstrues psychologism as maintaining that the laws of logic are, like the laws of association, about human minds. It is then easy for him to show that this is not the case, that, e.g., a correct statement of the principle of non-contradiction does not mention human beings or their minds. Meiland agrees that the laws of logic are not about human minds, but he takes psychologism as saying not that they are so, but that they are true by virtue of the nature of human mind: "they describe consequences of the way the mind works rather than the way the mind works." Meiland, in fact, suggests that Husserl may be right in that the laws of logic are about concepts or meanings, and yet psychologism may be right insofar as these concepts themselves are, at least partially, consequences of the nature of the human mind.

However, Meiland concludes his essay by raising two objections of his own against psychologism. In the first place, when a psychologistic theory of logic maintains that, with a different nature of mind, the laws of logic can be otherwise, the theory makes a judgment about what is possible. However, the only standard of possibility available derives from the present logical laws, which are precisely what, the theory says, could *possibly* be otherwise. For this last "possibly," the theory has no criterion.

Secondly, can the human mind, and so the laws of logic, change in such a manner that a proposition could be both true and false? If we gave up our concepts of 'truth', 'falsity', 'proposition', then we *would* have different laws of logic. But such a change does not permit a proposition to be both true and false. The new logic would not be a denial of the present logic, but totally unrelated to it. In fact, to say that the present logic would become false would be to make use of the present logic and its laws determining the laws of 'truth' and 'falsity'.

Meiland expects that psychologism may possibly be salvaged from these two objections. One attempt to salvage it is made by Remmel T. Nunn.[24] Nunn's attempt consists, in the first place, in using a functionalist theory of mind, such as has been advanced by Harman and Fodor. In such a theory, the mental states are defined in terms of the computational states of an automaton—those states which may be assigned a computational interpretation. But these internal states are determined by the physical properties of the organism (or of the automaton). Thus logical inference and physical causality are intertwined in a mental entity. Such a theory, Nunn argues, provides a support to psychologism, a stronger support, I believe, than either the traditional associationistic psychology or reductionistic physicalism could lend it. Furthermore, on such a theory, a machine may be so designed that it will consistently make a formal mistake M—mistake according to *our* present laws of logic—without ever being able to detect that M is a mistake. Nunn also suggests an account of conceptual change which is not as radical as Meiland ascribes to psychologism (and demonstrates to be unhelpful for the psychologistic theory of logic), but which is only a partial change in our present logic, such that the original system and the changed system partially overlap while being mutually inconsistent. He imagines a system in which the concepts of truth, falsity, and proposition are retained while the principle of non-contradiction is rejected, inasmuch as—in the system sketched by Nunn—"the perspective of the entity making the inference counts as a valid factor in the inferential process." An alternate logical system of such a kind is quite conceivable. The argument that the idea of 'possibility' is based on our present logical laws is supposed to have been disarmed by the machine analogy insofar as what is possible for the automaton is grounded in its internal computational states or innate structure.

While these considerations lend strength to psychologism, Føllesdal has argued that Husserl's refutations of psychologism all either beg the question or, in the long run, appeal to the idea of self-evidence (*Evidenz*). When Husserl argues[25] that the relativist's position that what is true for one may be false for another not only contradicts the sense of the word 'truth', but is absurd, for the same proposition cannot be both true and false, it is easy to see that Husserl *either* would simply be asserting, as against the relativist, that "truth" means absolute, non-relative truth or, in support of this assertion, he would have to—as in fact he does—appeal to the self-evidence of this understanding of "truth". Or, consider the following argument of Husserl:[26] the relativist's position amounts to the contradiction, "It is true that there is no truth." But, again, what the relativist really maintains is: "It is true$_1$ that there is no truth$_2$," where "true$_1$" = "taken for true by me" and true$_2$" = "absolutely true." Husserl apparently is saying that the relativist, when he affirms his own position, has to be affirming an absolute truth and so must be contradicting himself. But this the relativist need not do.

I will briefly consider these arguments, first those that defend psychologism and then those that are meant to demonstrate the impossibility of objectively refuting psychologism. To begin with the latter first, it is one thing to *convince* the psychologistic philosopher, another to refute him. Husserl recognizes that "refutation presupposes the leverage of certain self-evident, universally valid convictions," and that one cannot persuade the subjectivist and the sceptic. But refuting him is quite another thing. To say that in refuting the relativist one is making use of objective principles, and so is begging the issue, would not do. For the very idea of 'refutation', and not the absolutist's procedure, presupposes objectively valid argumentation. Strictly speaking, for the relativist, there is no 'refutation' not merely of his own position but of any position whatsoever. Saying, then, that in refuting the relativist one is making use of objectively valid principles is making a trivial point. Husserl's point, then, is that the relativist's own position contradicts the sense of his affirmation. If he is advancing a *theory*, his theory contradicts the very sense of 'theory' in general. To say that Husserl is thereby presupposing the validity of the principle of non-contradiction is to misconstrue the issue. The issue is not, insofar as the psychologistic logician is concerned, whether the principle of non-contradiction is valid. The psychologistic logician, insofar as he is a logician, accepts the principle, but insofar as his theory of logic is psychologism, gives a psychological theory of the origin of this principle. He therefore does not want to deny the validity of that principle. Husserl's point, then, is that the psychologistic logician's position involves a self-contradiction insofar as his theory contradicts the *sense* of 'theory' *in general*. Even psychologism *as a theory* has to be an objectively valid interconnection of propositions.

It should moreover be emphasized that what Husserl is defending in the *Prolegomena* is not a particular system of logic (to which there are alternate possible systems), but the very *idea* of pure logic, the *essence* of the logical *as such*. If every logical system can be formulated as an implication of the form 'If P, then T', where 'P' stands for the primitive undefined ideas, definitions, axiom set, and rules of formation and transformation and 'T' stands for the set of theorems in that system, then *this* If-then itself cannot be thematized within the system. The essence of the logical pertains precisely to this. No matter which system of logic one considers, in order to be a logic it must satisfy certain criteria, and these criteria define the idea of *possibility* involved in *possible* logics. Consider the egocentric logic sketched by Nunn, a logic in which the egocentric perspective of the entity making the inference counts as a valid factor in the inferential process. Now if this is to be a *logic*, its validity, i.e., the validity of its theorems, must have to be independent of the psychological vagaries of the inferring agents. If the system *cannot* accommodate such rules of inference (and theorems), then it would not be a *logic*. Withholding the name 'logic' is not, in that case, just an arbitrary decision on the part of the absolutist, but follows from the only concept of logic we have and is justified by the only way we are entitled to talk about logics.

It would not do to say that the relativist does not have the use of 'truth' in the absolutist's sense of that term, so that when he says, "It is true that there is no truth," what he means is, "I take-it-to-be-true that there is no absolute truth." It is of course the case that he does *not want* the concept of truth and wants to replace it by 'taken-to-be-true'. Quite apart from the problem that such replacement needs specifications such as "by whom" and "when," the real trouble with his contention is that the very concept of 'taken-to-be-true' implies the concept of true *simpliciter*. I take something to be true when I take it to be true *simpliciter*. Thus even if the relativist does not want to use the concept of 'true simpliciter', he uses one which indirectly refers to it. What I am suggesting is a sort of transcendental argument to the effect that the relativist cannot coherently state his position.

I think Meiland's distinction between the laws of association, which are *about* mental events, and the laws of logic, which, even on the psychologistic theory, are *not* about our minds, but *follow from* the nature of our minds, is important, but does not rescue psychologism from incoherence. For the idea of "following from" makes sense only if the logical principles are already assumed.

A functionalist theory of mind appears to avoid some of the pitfalls of the other, more common empiricist themes. A psychologistic theory of logic, which makes use of such a theory of the mind, avoids the two extremes of reductive physicalism and subjectivistic mentalism. Most of the anti-psychologistic arguments, whether of Frege or of Husserl, are directed against either of these two. It is easy to show that functionalism is immune to them. This is not the place to examine functionalism as a theory of mind. But as a theory of logic, in other words as a new variety of logical psychologism, it is worthless, for the construction of the functional theory, like that of any theory qua theory, implies precisely the sort of logical concepts whose explanation the theory would be giving. While the anti-psychologistic arguments are rendered ineffective, we would no longer have what Husserl and Frege would have called a psychologistic theory of logic. In fact, we would not have a theory of logic at all.

Føllesdal contends that Frege, as contrasted with Husserl, does not attempt to give an objectively valid refutation of psychologism, and, further, that Husserl, in formulating his refutations, makes use of allegedly self-evident concepts and principles, including the sense of the word 'truth'. I want to contend, however, that Frege does in fact give *arguments* against psychologism, and does not merely reject it as absurd. In an 1897 text, "Logic," Frege writes:

> If anyone tried to contradict the statement that what is true is true independently of our recognizing it as such, he would by his very assertion contradict what he had asserted; he would be in a similar position to the Cretan who said that all Cretans are liars.[27]

Furthermore, Frege argues, if something were true only for him who took it to be true, there would be no contradiction between the opinions of different persons. The person holding such a psychologistic theory would not then be in a position to contradict

the opposite view. His seeming assertions would really be interjec-
tions. "There would be no science, no error and no correction of
error." Frege obviously wants to draw absurd consequences from
the psychologistic theory, thereby claiming to refute the latter. In
doing this, he no less than Husserl falls back on the meaning of
'truth': the laws of logic, Frege asserts on various occasions, are "an
unfolding of the content of the word 'true'."

Another way of bringing out the same absurd consequence is
this: psychologism does not distinguish between the causes that
produce a belief and the grounds that justify it. In fact, for
psychologism, there are only causes, but no justification of beliefs,
which would put, Frege writes, a superstition on the same footing
as a scientific discovery.[28]

Frege thought that psychologism leads to the conclusion that
only subjective ideas exist, a position he regarded as incoherent.
Since an idea must be someone's idea, and since the subject whose
idea it is cannot itself be an idea, there must exist something that
is not a subjective idea.[29] Thus the very being of ideas entails the
existence of something that is not an idea, which psychologism
cannot accommodate within its theory.[30]

IV

Although Frege and Husserl agreed in their opposition to
psychologism as a theory of *logic* (despite their differences as to
whether psychologism could be logically refuted), they held very
different views about the nature of psychology itself and, more importantly, about the concept of 'subjectivity'. Especially in
Husserl's case, a correct understanding of his attitude toward psychology is necessary if we are to be able to assess the work of the
frequently voiced complaint about Husserl's "relapse" into
psychologism after a brief spell of (Fregean) anti-psychologism in
the *Prolegomena*.

To what extent their attitudes toward psychology decisively
influenced their theories of knowledge we shall see in chapter 4. It
is indeed difficult to say if Frege had a preference as regards what
psychology should be like. From his rather scanty statements about
psychology it seems that he thought of it as a *descriptive* science of
actual mental processes, which he contrasts with logic, which is a
normative science of how we ought to think.[31] The laws of psychology are like laws of nature: they are universals in the mental

realm.[32] Mental processes happen in accordance with these laws. The laws of psychology are guiding principles of thought in the sense that "they give an average, like statements about 'how it is that good digestion occurs in man', or 'how one speaks grammatically', or 'how one dresses fashionably'."[33] But no such law has unrestricted authority, and any such law may well change with time. There is no reason to believe that Frege wanted to belittle psychology as a science. What he wanted to reject outright is any intrusion of psychological explanations into the domains of logic and mathematics. I believe he would have agreed with Husserl that insofar as psychology itself is a science, it must make use of logical principles: it must distinguish between what is true and what is simply taken to be true.

Husserl's views about psychology are far more explicit and well worked out. In fact, as unsparing a critic of psychologism as he became, his concern with psychology as a science yet continued to grow. It was far from his intention ever to reject psychology as such, or even to reject outright the relevance of psychology in general to foundational questions.[34] The critique of psychologism in the *Prolegomena* was a rejection of claims of *empirical* and *genetic* psychology to provide the foundations for logic and knowledge. As early as the "Selbstanzeige"[35] he wrote for the *Prolegomena*, as we have pointed out earlier in this essay, he characterizes phenomenology as descriptive psychology as contrasted with genetic psychology. In about 1900 or 1901, then, Husserl thought that phenomenology in the sense of a descriptive psychology could clarify the fundamental concepts of logic and knowledge. Thus in the first edition of the *Logical Investigations*, he writes, in response to an objection ("What then is the point of the whole battle against psychologism?"):

> The necessity of *this* sort of psychological foundation of pure logic, i.e., a strictly descriptive one, cannot lead us into error regarding the mutual independence of the two sciences, logic and psychology. For pure description is merely a preparatory step towards theory, not theory itself. . . . It is *not the full science of psychology that serves as a foundation for pure logic*, but certain classes of descriptions. . . .

He speaks of such descriptions as being antecedent to theoretical psychology itself, descriptions which are "disembarrassed of all theoretical psychological interest."[36]

About the year 1903 Husserl seems to have rejected this conception of phenomenology.[37] In the introduction to the second edition, he replaces the paragraph containing the sentences just quoted with a completely different paragraph, in which he writes:

> if psychology is given its old meaning, phenomenology is not descriptive psychology: its peculiar 'pure' description, its contemplation of pure essences on a basis of exemplary individual intuitions of experiences (often freely *imagined* ones), and its descriptive fixation of the contemplated essences into pure concepts, is no empirical, scientific description.[38]

Phenomenology is *eidetic* psychology of pure experiences, of perceptions, judgments, feelings *as such*, and not as states of animal organisms. If a large part of Husserl's argument against psychologism centered around the distinction between sciences of facts and sciences of essences, then *that* argument would not count against the claim of an eidetic psychology of pure experiences to provide clarification of the fundamental concepts of logic and knowledge. At this point, the contrast between Brentano and Husserl is instructive. Brentano was assured by Husserl that the charge of psychologism was not directed against him. This was not a mere attempt on Husserl's part to please his acknowledged master; Husserl was being honest. The *Prolegomena* was directed against empirical-genetic psychology. Brentano's psychology, though empirical, was descriptive, not genetic. Even as empirical, it was of a different sort than the psychology the psychologistic logicians made use of. Unlike most empirical psychologies[39] Brentano's did appeal to apodictic or necessary laws about the nature of thinking and feeling, arrived at by a sort of intuitive induction from particular cases.[40] While Brentano was using the method of intuitive induction, Husserl was speaking of 'intuition of essences' (*Wesenschau*). The difference between them is not as great as it may at first appear to be.[41]

There is another aspect of the descriptive, eidetic psychology as conceived of by Husserl—this, too, deriving from Brentano. Such a psychology must be *intentional*. It shall describe the peculiar intentionalities proper to each type of mental act, and, in accordance with Husserl's own understanding of intentionality, shall bring out the noesis-noema correlations that pervade all conscious life. From this, the step toward a transcendental phenomenological psychology is, for Husserl, compelling and almost inevitable. Psychology, as Husserl recognized, can provide a way to transcendental phenomenology, but only if psychology is correctly understood as descriptive, eidetic, and intentional.

V

From this brief account of their attitudes toward psychology, we can gather their very different understanding of the subjective. At least since the time of Kant, one is accustomed to the distinction between psychological subjectivity and transcendental subjectivity. The psychologically subjective is what belongs to or is part of an individual's mental life and is thus private to him, something no one else can share, of which he alone is the bearer, and about whose *content* universal truths are not possible. What Frege generally calls subjective, which he often lumps together under the words 'idea' and 'presentation', is precisely subjective in this psychological sense. Both external things, which can be perceived in common and need no bearer in order to be, and thoughts, which also can be apprehended in common and exist on their own, are, then, sharply distinguished from the inner, psychologically subjective, ideas.[42] Of Frege's three worlds, the world of the inner alone is subjective, but it is subjective in the psychological sense.

Other philosophers, including Kant and Husserl, have recognized a quite different order of subjectivity, one that is not only not opposed to objectivity but, on the contrary, is regarded as the foundation of objectivity. The transcendentally subjective, though subjective in the sense of belonging to the (human) mind, is yet *shared* by all rational beings in common. It is the common structure, not the merely formal aspect, of all rational minds, a structure which alone makes intersubjective discourse possible, and is thus a necessary, if not sufficient, condition of the possibility of an objective world and of objective science. Husserl shared with the Kantians this conception of transcendental subjectivity, although in his thinking it underwent very significant and interesting transformations. It would be pointless to ask if Frege recognized such a notion had it not been for the alleged fact that Frege did consider himself to be a neo-Kantian of a sort.[43] In fact, in *Grundlagen* §26, Frege writes:

It is in this way that I understand objective to mean what is independent of our sensation, intuition and imagination, and of all construction of mental pictures out of memories of earlier sensations, but not what is independent of the reason,—for what are things independent of reason?[44]

The text clearly suggests that by "Reason" Frege understands something close to what Kantians and Husserl understand by 'transcendental subjectivity'.[45] But it must be conceded that Frege never brings this concept to bear on his ontology. Insofar as he ascribes to mankind a common stock of thoughts ("einen gemeinsamen Schatz von Gedanken"), this common stock may well be regarded as his "equivalent" of the Kantian "Reason." The implicit Kantianism of his theory of knowledge we shall discuss in chapter 3.

One more question needs to be asked here in connection with Frege's concept of subjectivity. Did Frege have a concept of intentionality? Linke[46] and Bergmann[47] think that he had. Linke ascribes to Frege, particularly in the light of "Der Gedanke," a Brentano-like view of the mental, and Bergmann regards Frege as "the first who clearly saw the logical problem of intentionality." Linke refers particularly to the text cited above: "One sees a thing, one has an idea, one apprehends or thinks a thought." What Bergmann has in mind is Frege's discussion of belief contexts and indirect discourse. It appears to me that if for a mental act to be intentional means (1) that it has an object, then not only would *almost* every philosopher accept the Brentano thesis, but that thesis itself would be bereft of any special significance. Brentano's point was not merely that every mental act has an object in that commonly acceptable sense, but something more: for one thing, (2) *in* any mental 'phenomenon', there is a directedness toward an object and, for another, (3) this directedness is not a relation proper inasmuch as it may obtain even when one of the terms, viz., the object toward which the act is directed, does not exist. The directedness is rather an intrinsic feature of the act. Even this thesis of Brentano's lacked an important aspect: namely, an explanation of why a particular act is directed toward a particular object and toward none other. In other words, (4) an account was needed in terms of some intrinsic structure of the act (without presupposing a prior account of the structure of its object) which makes an act directed toward its object and none other. Frege's theory of *sense* had all the potentialities of providing such an account, insofar as the Fregean sense contains the mode of givenness of the referent.

But since the Fregean senses remain attached to expressions, words, and sentences, or rather to *names*, they at most provide an account of how a name refers to whatever it is a name of. The mental acts are intentional only by proxy. In fact, as Bergmann himself acknowledges,[48] his philosophy of mind is not explicitly worked out; he says very little about the mental *acts* in general — even in the later papers where some concern with mental acts emerges. I would therefore agree with Bergmann that Frege was probably the first to see the *logical* problems of *intensionality*, but he did not appropriate this into a theory of *intentionality*, as Husserl did. The mental act, the senses, the word, and the object — all remain loosely connected, in fact disjoined.

Frege's remarkably sophisticated logical theory and semantics remain in sharp contrast with a rather naive philosophy of mind. And, yet, this latter was precisely Husserl's central concern: how is it possible for subjective acts, temporally and egologically individuated particulars, to have objective senses? The metaphor of 'grasping' provides the initial, and, as a first approximation, correct description. But one would still want to know what is involved in this grasping.

Frege certainly shows an awareness of the problematic character of this 'grasping' when he writes:

> But still the grasping of this law [the law of Gravitation] is a mental process! Yes, indeed, but it is a process which takes place on the very confines of the mental and which for that reason *cannot* be completely understood from a purely psychological standpoint. For in grasping the law something comes into view whose nature is no longer mental in the proper sense, namely the thought; and this process is perhaps the most mysterious of all.[49]

Frege adds in a footnote to this text: "I should say that this question of grasping thoughts and recognizing them to be true is still far from being grasped in all its difficulty."[50] Compare this with Husserl's statement in the Foreword to the first edition of the *Logical Investigations:* "I felt myself more and more pushed towards general critical reflections on the essence of logic, and on the relationship, in particular, between the subjectivity of knowing and the objectivity of the content known."[51] In the draft of the Foreword to the second edition, he speaks of the dimension of "mystery" about the relation between the being in itself of the ideal sphere and consciousness—a mystery which, Husserl continues, remains untouched by the anti-psychologistic argumentations and can be illuminated only by a different sort of inquiry, namely the phenomenological.

VI

Two philosophers—one a senior contemporary of Husserl, Paul Natorp, and another a young follower, Martin Heidegger—insisted on the provisional character of the anti-psychologism of the *Prolegomena*. Drawing attention to the oppositions that Husserl draws between the psychological and the logical, Natorp wrote:

> The material, empirical, psychological, i.e., the 'real', remains an uncomprehended, irrational surd; the question about the *relation*, the inner, epistemological and also the *logical* bond between the two is not at all raised, but with their sharp and pure *separation* the problem is laid to rest. And therefore . . . the reader is left with a certain logical dissatisfaction. One follows the dramatically tense struggle between the two opponents, and yet does not see, where precisely is the root of their opposition, what precisely is that which makes this life and death battle necessary; but therewith an exact reciprocal relationship, even an inseparable belonging together between the two shows itself more and more . . . [52]

Natorp's suggestion is that "A bond, a *logical* connection *must* be set up between the super-temporal being of the logical and its temporal actualization in the experience of the mind. . . ." By "actualization," Natorp means not a "mystical, metaphysical act," but "a strictly intelligble logical transition from one mode of consideration to another, which ultimately was already implicit in it." Natorp's conclusion is: "The drama must be led towards this climax, till then the curtain should not fall."[53]

In his Marburg lectures on logic Heidegger expounds Husserl's anti-psychologistic arguments in some detail and with great appreciation. He regards the *Prolegomena* as an indispensable and important step toward understanding the nature of the logic.[54] But the absolute separation of the real (i.e., the temporal act of thinking) and the ideal (i.e., the non-temporal content of thought, or meaning), Heidegger notes,[55] makes it impossible to account for the actual, living thought. Husserl did not ask about that entity which does not merely bridge the gap between the two, the real and the ideal, but rather, in its own original unity, makes that distinction possible.[56] Obviously, Heidegger is suggesting here his idea of *Dasein* as being that entity. But he does, however, recognize that Husserl is asking a somewhat related question: what constitutes the mental qua mental? The thesis of intentionality implies that the intentional act is *not* the merely real, inner, experience, it is *ab initio* directed outwards and has an ideal sense. Thus, the structure of intentionality provides the unity *within* which the real-ideal distinction is made. This, however, is not a radical enough step for Heidegger.[57]

Husserl was keenly aware of the problem to which Natorp and Heidegger draw attention. In an entry in his diary, referring to those early years, he wrote:

> peinigte mich die unbegreiflich fremden Welten: die Welt des rein logischen und die Welt des Aktbewusstseins, wie ich heute sagen wurde, des phänomenologischen und auch psychologischen. Ich wusste sie nicht in eins zu setzen und doch mussten sie zueinander Beziehung haben und eine innere Einheit bilden.[58]

Husserl's final solution, in the form of his transcendental logic, sides neither with Natorp nor with Heidegger. While for my present purpose it is not necessary to go into that part of the story, I have tried to show why Husserl, while never retracting the anti-psychologism of the *Prolegomena*, could not rest at that point, but had to move on toward a sort of transcendental philosophy, and indeed why he never relapsed into psychologism.

VII

On various occasions, in his later writings, Husserl looks back at the anti-psychologism of the *Prolegomena*. However, it is only in the *Formal and Transcendental Logic*[59] that he makes a fresh contribution to the question of psychologism. In this section, I want to consider that contribution, which has two parts. First, Husserl now states the achievements of the *Prolegomena* in a somewhat novel manner in an attempt to make it consistent with the idea of a transcendental grounding of formal logic. The other new element is the introduction of the concept of 'transcendental psychologism.'

(a) As regards the first: after reiterating the point that the *Prolegomena* was concerned not with psychologism in general (i.e., with reduction of all objectivities to psychological genesis), but only with logical psychologism (understood as "the psychologizing of the irreal significational formations that are the theme of logic"[60]), Husserl proceeds to give a new formulation of the argument *for* the psychologistic philosophy of logic (§57a), and a not-quite-novel formulation of his own point against it (§57b). The motive for logical psychologism is now said to lie in the fact that such entities as judgments, sets, cardinal numbers, etc., are products of our mental life, and that these products make their appearance within the inner life of the thinking subject. Such a formation as a judgment or an inference takes shape "within" one's conscious life step by step; it is a phenomenon appearing in internal experience, in the act-consciousness itself. The *Prolegomena*'s account of psychologism does not contain, it should be noted, such a statement of its position; such a statement could only be possible *after* one has assumed the stance of an *immanent* descriptive psychology. The emphasis is not on genesis of the products in mental acts, but on the fact that these products "appear" within the thinker's mental life.

However, this argument is muddled, for the alleged description is simply mistaken. Entities such as a judgment, a set, or a number "appear" with the same claim to transcendence, with the same sense of "objectivity," as things of the external world. They are not only "seen," but are capable of being reidentified as being the same, just as external things—judgment, the same set, the same number—are. There is thus a transcendence belonging to every sort of object as against the consciousness of them.

Here in the *Formal and Transcendental Logic*, Husserl recognizes that the entities of logic are indeed productions, but he also cautions against a very natural misunderstanding of that locution (§63). What is produced in an act of judging is not a *real* mental entity, but an *irreal* entity, an entity that can then be intersubjectively identified, recognized, and reidentified. Once produced, a judgment, by virtue of the very *sense* of its being, acquires a transcendence, it "transcends the current living evidence" in which it actually becomes self-given (§73). Psychologism fails to take note of the sense of being of the logical entities, of the fact that they are "always-identifiable senses." Transcendental logic, while recognizing this *irreducible* phenomenon, also asks how such significations are constituted, how they come to evident self-givenness, in the flow of intentional life of consciousness. It thus saves whatever element of truth there *could* be in psychologism.

What then did the *Prolegomena* achieve, in the context of such a transcendental logic? In order to understand Husserl's self-interpretation of this point, we need to recall that for him every science has *three* thematic spheres (§66). For one thing, a science has its *province*, which constitutes its theme in the most proper sense. But then, to every science there also belongs what may be called *its* logic, its own methods and principles of self-criticism. If pure logic is the universal science of theory qua theory, every science relates to such a universal logic by its own specifications. It is in this sense that one can speak of the logic of physics or of history. Husserl calls it 'analytic criticism of cognition', and such a logic constitutes the second thematic sphere. Thus far most philosophers of science will go along with him. Husserl adds, however, a third thematic sphere that, like the second, is critical but that unlike it, relates not to the formal logical principles but to the intentional, subjective life that "corresponds" to each province. Transcendental criticism of cognition, as Husserl calls it, will lay bare the hidden intentional acts which constitute the first two thematic spheres of the science. Only such a criticism can be radical criticism, as is demanded by the very idea of science. Now, we can say that what the anti-psychologism of the *Prolegomena* did achieve was to have exhibited the specific *province* of pure analytic logic in its purity and its ideal uniqueness, by freeing it from naturalistic misinterpretations of empirical, genetic psychologies. The proper thematic field of logic is thereby made visible, along with the nature of the analytic self-criticism that attaches to its own province. But this result should by no means be misconstrued as a demonstration of the autonomy and self-sufficiency of analytic logic,[61] nor should it be taken to rule out a "transcendental criticism" of pure formal logic, which would bring to light the intentionalities constituting the formal logical objectivities.

Thus understood, a refutation of psychologism and of all naturalistic epistemologies is not only not inconsistent with, but is a precondition of, genuine transcendental philosophy. If the task of transcendental philosophy is to show the constitution of objective meanings in intentional acts, it first needs to be established that there are such objective senses.[62]

(b) The second new idea, as I said above, is the introduction of 'transcendental psychologism'. He does not say much about it, but it appears that he is led to it by his concern not merely with refuting psychology, but with a more difficult problem: why is psychologism a constant possibility and temptation? I think Husserl came to realize that a logical refutation of psychologism does not dispel, once and for all, the nagging feeling that after all a judgment, a thought, a meaning, cannot but be a real mental experience, a psychological product, or that the logical and the psychological must at some level coincide. Why this temptation, even if one sees that the very *sense* of the being of logical entities is the sense of an irreal being, and that such an entity could not be "in" someone's mind in the psychological sense? Ultimately, for Husserl, this is due to the *parallelism* between empirical, psychological subjectivity and transcendental subjectivity.[63] It is this parallelism that explains why transcendental grounding of the logical would be misconstrued as psychological origin. The *possibility* of psychologism, then, is due not to a simple philosophical error but to the fact that the empirical and the transcendental are indeed different "interpretations" of one and the same consciousness.[64]

CHAPTER 3

Theory of Sense

The two points on which Husserl and Frege came closest to agreement were their anti-psychologism and their distinction between sense and reference. The two are intimately connected. Rejection of psychologism is also rejection of any psychological theory of sense and reference. For both Husserl and Frege, then, neither the sense nor the reference of an expression is a mental entity (unless the word is a mental word, in which case the reference, but not the sense, is mental). However, anti-psychologism is consistent with the theories (such as those found in Russell or the *Tractatus*) that identify meaning with reference. Neither Husserl nor Frege would find such theories acceptable. Both desired, in addition to the reference, and in addition as well to any mental image or association that a word may evoke, an objective sense.

Husserl's terminology is different from Frege's. What Frege calls *'Sinn'*, he calls *'Bedeutung'*; for Frege's *'Bedeutung'*, he uses *'Gegenstand'*. The exact translation of *'Bedeutung'* has been a subject of some controversy;[1] for this reason Husserl's *'Gegenstand'* is a better choice. I shall, however, render Frege's *Sinn* (and Husserl's *'Bedeutung'*) as 'sense', and Frege's *'Bedeutung'* (and Husserl's *'Gegenstand'*) as 'reference'. By this I do not mean to prejudge any of the issues in Frege exegesis nor do I claim that 'reference' may not indeed mislead. But I believe that it is only if we are aware of the risks we are taking that we may be able to prevent errors in interpretation that are likely to arise from a faulty translation. In order to avoid one such, let us make a distinction which Frege unfortunately does not make. 'Reference' may mean either the function of referring or the thing to which a sign refers. Let us call the former 'reference' and the latter 'referent'.

Frege holds the view that all names have their senses as distinguished from their references. The category 'name' includes, for him, ordinary proper names, definite descriptions, indexicals, and expressions formed by any of these. How is the idea of 'sense' to be introduced, assuming that what we have available to us are only external and internal entities all of which are referents? In order to be able to understand Frege's reasons, we may approach his thesis both historically and logically.

Historically considered, Frege had not made the sense-reference distinction in the *Begriffsschrift* and the *Grundlagen*. In the *Begriffsschrift* §2, he distinguished between the judgment stroke, the content stroke, and the content of possible judgment. In the sign

 A,

the small vertical stroke at the left end of the horizontal stroke expresses 'assertion'; it is the judgment stroke. Without the vertical line, the horizontal line by itself expresses a "mere combination of ideas" which is not, however, being asserted: it is the content stroke. 'A' signifies an assertable content, a content of possible judgment. Later on Frege tells us[2] that the 'content of possible judgment' combines both sense (i.e., the thought expressed by 'A') and reference (i.e., the truth value of A). Since according to the so-called context principle "only in a proposition have the words really a meaning,"[3] Frege must have arrived at the idea of the sense expressed by a declarative sentence before he extended the thesis to names and predicate expressions. Once the concept of "the content of possible judgment" is split into two—the thought expressed by the sentence and its truth value—'thinking' and 'judging' can be clearly distinguished, the former being grasping of the thought, the latter being recognition of its truth value.

Once we have the notion of 'thought' as what is expressed by a declarative sentence, we can have a good argument that names occurring in such a sentence must also have their senses. One such argument is the following. (1) An object cannot be part of a thought in the same manner as the proper name of that object is part of the corresponding sentence. "Mont Blanc with its masses of snow and ice is not part of the thought that Mont Blanc is more than 4,000 meters high."[4] All we can say is, there must be a part of that thought which corresponds to Mont Blanc. This is the sense of the proper name 'Mont Blanc' whose referent is the mountain Mont Blanc. To quote Frege:

> something further must be associated with the proper name, something which is different from the object designated and which is essential to the thought of the sentence in which the proper name occurs. I call it the sense of the proper name. As the proper name is part of the sentence, so its sense is part of the thought.[5]

The same is true of the other part of the sentence, i.e., the predicate expression.

There is a different reasoning in support of the same conclusion.[6] (2) One may ask, if the object itself is not a component of the thought, is the object at all necessary for the sentence to express a thought? A sentence containing the name 'Odysseus' does express a thought, even if the name 'Odysseus' does not name anyone. Suppose that later on it is found that the name 'Odysseus', as it occurs in that sentence, does in fact designate someone. This discovery would not in the least alter the thought content expressed by the sentence. Consequently, the name has a sense associated with it that is different from, and independent of, its reference and that is what contributes to the thought expressed by the sentence of which the name is a part.

Arguments (1) and (2) assume, but do not themselves establish, that a sentence has its sense quite apart from its reference. Assuming that there is a sentential sense, which is the thought expressed by a sentence, arguments (1) and (2) purport to prove that the names occurring in the sentence must have their own senses: what they contribute to the total sense of the sentence. The next argument, which Frege often gives, is also not independent of that assumption:

(3) It is frequently the case that the same object has many different names, and yet these names are not simply interchangeable. The sentence 'Mont Blanc is over 4,000 meters high' expresses a sense that is different from that expressed by 'The highest mountain in Europe is over 4,000 meters high'. It follows that 'Mont Blanc' and 'The highest mountain in Europe', although naming the same object, have different senses.[7]

A form of this argument which dispenses with the assumption that sentences have their sense is this:

(3') Although 'Mont Blanc' and 'The highest mountain in Europe' name the same object, substitution of the one for the other does not preserve the truth value of the sentences in which they occur. A true sentence, 'Smith believed that Mont Blanc is over 4,000 meters high', may not, by substitution of 'the highest mountain in Europe' for 'Mont Blanc', result in a true sentence. It follows that something else attaches to each of the two names, which contributes to the composition of what is the object of Smith's belief. This argument, to get off the ground, does not presuppose Frege's particular theory of truth values (as referents of sentences). It also does not presuppose the thesis that the object of belief in each case is not the object, not an objective complex, but the thought expressed by the sentential clause. Indeed, it purports to prove both that the object of belief is a *thought* and that the sense expressed by the name occurring in the sentential clause following the belief verb contributes to the composition of that thought. It may, however, be maintained that although in order to get off the ground (3') does not need to assume that sentences have their senses (i.e., express thoughts), it first proves that thesis before proceeding to prove that the names occurring in the sentences have their own senses. This uneasiness is somewhat lesser in the case of the celebrated argument in the opening paragraphs of "Sinn und Bedeutung":

(4) Although the two identity statements

"Mont Blanc = Mont Blanc" and
"Mont Blanc = The highest mountain in Europe"

are such that if the second is true, the first can be derived from it by substitution, they do not have the same *cognitive value*. The former is quite uninformative, being a substitution instance of the principle of identity. The latter is clearly informative. This difference in cognitive value of the two statements is due to the fact that although the two expressions 'Mont Blanc' and 'the highest mountain in Europe' have an identical referent, they have different *senses*, or, rather, that with regard to which they differ from each other, apart from their physical shapes (which are irrelevant for the present purpose), is the sense. The senses involved account for the differences in cognitive value. This argument does not presuppose the idea of sentential sense. The idea of cognitive value, which it does make use of, pertains to the statements rather than to the thoughts expressed by the sentences.

The fact that, of the five arguments given to prove that names have their senses as distinguished from their references, only one is independent of the thesis of sentential sense, shows that the so-called context principle was decisive for Frege. That he did not quite abandon the principle in "Sinn und Bedeutung" is attested by the fact that arguments (1) through (3) continue to appear in post-humously published writings after 1892.[8] However, one cannot deny that Frege's theory contained an unresolved tension between the context principle and the thesis that names as such have their senses. If Frege held the view that the sentential sense is composed of the senses of the component parts of the sentence, then the tension is between this principle of composition and the context principle. One may seek to dispel this tension by saying that the principle of composition is a misleading designation for the idea that the sentential sense is *analyzable into* —not composed of—the sense of each part. This, however, is not of much help, for the whole, i.e., the sentential sense, can be reconstituted out of those part senses. What would in any case jar with the context principle is the thesis that names have senses which, like their referents, are saturated, in no need for completion, and unlike the senses as well as the referents of predicate expressions.

Since the thesis about sentential sense is such an integral part of the Fregean theory of sense, one should ask how Frege arrives at it. It would not do to say that that thesis, as well as the overall idea of sense, is required in order to assign objects to indirect discourse verbs ("He said that . . .") and verbs in intensional contexts ("He believes that . . ."). This would not do, for, as Dummett has pointed out,[9] unless we already have at our disposal the idea of sense, the theory that senses are objects in those sorts of discourse cannot be introduced, and one who does not countenance senses would look for other kinds of entities—linguistic entities, for example,—to serve that purpose.

Frege took truth to be nonrelative, objective, and the same for all. It could not, therefore, he thought, pertain to a sentence or to a mental state; the former is relative to a language, the latter is private to a person. Accordingly, truth (or falsity) can pertain[10] only to a timeless entity which is other than a sentence and also not a mental experience. This timeless entity is of a "third" sort: neither external nor inner. This is the *sense* expressed by a sentence. Truth pertains to a sense.

In arriving at his theory of sense, Frege was also answering the question: what does understanding an expression involve? What is it that the mind *grasps* when one understands an expression? To understand a sentence is not yet to understand its truth or falsity. To understand a name is not to determine its referent. For Frege, it is to grasp its sense. In this respect, Dummett is right in saying that the concept of sense is an epistemic concept.[11]

Both these answers are vulnerable, and need a considerable amount of defense, which this essay is not meant to provide. To say the least, the two are at least as defensible as any theory of meaning I know of. The strength of Frege's theory lies in the rather *implicit* phenomenology on which it is based: the distinctions between (i) merely having a presentation, (ii) perceiving an external object, (iii) understanding or thinking, (iv) judging, and (v) asserting. For a fuller development of this phenomenology and resolution of some of the tensions which persist in Frege, we need to turn to Husserl.

II

And, yet, Husserl's *arguments* in support of his sense-reference distinction are not as fully developed as Frege's. The basic insights, however, are the same. Not unlike Frege, he appeals to the fact[12] that expressions having different meanings may have the same reference. But, unlike Frege, he argues that expressions having the same meaning may yet have different objects. His examples for the former are: 'the victor at Jena'— 'the vanquished at Waterloo', 'the equilateral triangle'—'the equiangular triangle'. For the latter sort of case, he gives the example of the expression 'a horse', which, although having the same meaning in whatever context it occurs, refers in 'Bucephalus is a horse' to Bucephalus and in 'That carthorse is a horse' to the carthorse. He proceeds to tell us that the same is true of all general names, i.e., names having an extension.[13]

Indeed, there is little difference between Husserl and Frege with regard to names, other than proper names. The difference chiefly concerns the predicate expressions. Husserl holds what may be called the standard view: namely, that a predicate expression such

as "a horse" has for its sense the concept 'horse', and for its reference the *extension*, i.e., the indefinite range of its possible applica-
tion. This indefinite range of objects is delimited to the individual
referred to by 'Bucephalus' in 'Bucephalus is a horse'.[14] Frege, on
the other hand, regarded the concept itself as the reference of the
predicate expression, and distinguished from it its sense. He
thought he needed this revision—as he explains in a letter to
Husserl[15]—in order to account for the fact that a concept may be
empty, may not have anything falling under it, and yet be scientifically useful. With his extensional concept of science, he felt
satisfied that the reference of the predicate expression is assured
even if the concept is empty. However, he had to pay the price for
this in two ways: first, Frege never could clarify what, if it is not
the concept, the sense of a predicate expression is; secondly, the
reference of a predicate expression is, in his thesis, automatically
guaranteed. Even an inconsistent concept is, for him, admissible in
science, as he argues in a 1906 paper,[16] for otherwise one could
never avail oneself of indirect proof. It is understandable, then, why
in Fregean semantics expressions with identical sense could not
have different references, for in each case 'a horse' has the same
reference (the concept 'horse') as well as the same sense. Even if
you take the reference to be the extension (and not the concept),
Husserl's point is difficult to substantiate, for 'a horse' always has
the same extension. What Husserl says is that on one occasion it
'presents' Bucephalus, and on the other the carthorse. This is indeed a very peculiar sense of 'reference'. The expression 'a horse' as
such does not have shifting reference, but in different judgments it
is used to characterize different members of its extension. It is also
obvious that Husserl has not produced examples of expressions
having the same sense but different tokens of the same expression
type.

With regard to whole (declarative) sentences, the differences between Frege's and Husserl's positions are also pronounced. Frege's
view is that a sentence expresses a thought (which is its sense) and
refers to, or designates, one of the two: the True or the False, depending upon whether it is true or false. The latter part of the
thesis—namely, that sentences refer to truth values and, there
being only two truth values, all true sentences have the same reference, as do all false sentences—in spite of the rather strange ontology that is implied, succeeds in achieving a remarkable simplicity

of interpretation for propositional logic. Moreover, it obviates the need for admitting facts into one's ontology. In any case, in his later writings, Frege appears not to have made much use of this part of the thesis. Excepting therefore its relevance for the conception of logic, this thesis may not be a *significant* point of difference between Frege and Husserl. Husserl held a less controversial position: a sentence expresses a proposition (which is its sense) and *refers to*: (i) in one interpretation, the object referred by the subject term, which is *the object about which* something is being said, and (ii), in another interpretation, the fact, the *Sachlage*, to which the total sentence stands in a relation analogous to that of a name and the named.[17] Thus a sentence has an object-about-which, and the fact being referred to—both to be distinguished from the proposition it expresses. To take Husserl's example, the two sentences 'A is greater than B' and 'B is smaller than A' express different thoughts (i.e., propositions), are *about*[18] different objects (the former about 'A' and the latter about 'B'), but refer to the same fact.

Is Husserl's 'proposition' the same as Frege's 'thought'? It would help to know if for Frege 'A is greater than B' and 'B is smaller than A' express the *same* thought (where 'A' and 'B' are not variables but constants, i.e., names). My own inclination is to say, 'yes'. We know that active and passive voice constructions may express the same thought. 'B and A' and 'A and B' have the same sense, so also do 'not (A and B)' and 'not (B and A)', and 'A and A' and 'A'.[19] The criterion of sameness that he employs in this context is given in these sentences from a letter to Husserl:

> In order to decide whether the sentence A expresses the same thought as the sentence B, the following seems to me to be the only possible means, whereby I assume that neither of the two sentences contains a logically evident sense-component. If, namely, both the assumption that the content of A is false and that of B is true and the assumption that the content of A is true and that of B is false, lead to logical contradiction without it being necessary to determine whether the content of A or that of B is true or false and without using other than purely logical laws, then nothing can belong to the content of A, so far as it is capable of being true or false, which did not also belong to the content of B.[20]

In other words, 'A' and 'B' would, in that case, express the same *thought*.

We do not know what precise questions Husserl had raised in his letter to which Frege was replying. We do know, however, that Frege was responding to Husserl's remarks about equipollent or *gleichwertig* sentences. It is most likely that Husserl wanted to find a difference in sense even where two sentences are equipollent. Frege obviously does not feel the need for this. According to Frege's criterion, 'A is greater than B' and 'B is smaller than A' are equipollent; the assumption that one of them is true and the other false does indeed lead to contradiction. Consequently, they express the same *thought*. But they do not, according to Husserl, express the same *proposition*.[21] It appears, then, that Husserl's 'proposition' is more finely individuated than Frege's 'thought'. Frege's 'thought', as well as the criterion of its sameness, is defined to serve the restricted purposes of Frege's extensional, truth-functional logic. Any further differentiation, if redundant for purposes of this logic, is for Frege unimportant. Husserl has a more liberal concept of sentential sense (which still *excludes* what Frege would call 'coloring' and 'force' and contains nothing but objectively graspable and communicable content), but he needs some way of carving out of it the Fregean thought if he is to succeed in giving a theory of logic. The *problem* of propositional identity comes to the center of his attention in *Formal and Transcendental Logic*.

Frege, as is well known, ascribes the following characteristics to what he calls thought. Thoughts are *objective*. A thought does not belong to the person who thinks it. It is *impersonal*. It is not generated, but only grasped, by the act of thinking. Even false thoughts are independent of the thinker. They are independent not only of thinkers, but also of language. Only for them the *question of truth* arises. They are *eternal* and *immutable*. So if true, they are timelessly so. Also, thoughts are *complete* entities. They are not, as such, asserted, although assertion, like any other act, may attach to them. Thoughts, though not real (i.e., tangible and spatiotemporal), are *actual* in a rather special sense; they may, through their grasping, act upon us, but not we upon them. Husserl's sentential meanings are also objective,[22] timeless, unchanging,[23] and language-independent;[24] truth and falsity pertain to them primarily.[25] They are as such unasserted, for Husserl as well. Acts of differing qualities may have the same act-matter (in the language of the *Logical Investigations*); the same noematic sense may be accompanied by different thetic qualities (in the language of the

Ideas). False judgmental senses have as much being, in the region of senses, as true ones.[26]

What, then, is Husserl's 'fact' over and above the 'true thought', which is what Frege regards as fact?[27] Husserl discusses the concepts of fact and proposition in great detail in both the *Formal and Transcendental Logic*[28] and *Experience and Judgment*.[29] The brief exposition given below makes use of both the texts. Husserl uses and wants to distinguish between two words, '*Sachlage*' and '*Sachverhalt*', both of which may be rendered 'fact'. (His use of '*Tatsache*' is ambiguous in this regard. Use of '*Tatsache*' in the opening chapter of *Ideas I* is misleading.) If 'A > B' and 'B < A' refer to the same *Sachlage*, they state different *Sachverhalten*. The same *Sachlage* is *explicated* by the two judgments in different ways, so that two different syntactical objectivities are constituted by the two acts. These syntactical objectivities are the *Sachverhalten*, which are the objective correlates of the two judgments but which are not objectified in them. The that-clause 'That A > B' *names* not the *Sachlage* but the *Sachverhalt*. The perceptual statement 'This is white', then, is *about* the thing designated by 'this', refers to a *Sachlage* (which is being receptively apprehended), has a syntactical objectivity, i.e., a *Sachverhalt* or state of affairs, like its correlate (which is named by 'That this is white'.). The sentential sense is a proposition, considered apart from the question of its truth or falsity, which Husserl also equates with the state of affairs *supposed as such*. When this proposition is established as true, i.e., when the empty meaning intention (which is the proposition in the strict sense) is fulfilled, we have the *Sachverhalt* or the state of affairs itself. The "state of affairs itself," then, is the idea of the completely fulfilled propositional sense. To say that a state of affairs is actual is to say that the propositional sense is true. The straightforward act of judging is *not directed toward* either the *Sachlage* or the *Sachverhalt*. The *Sachlage* is being referred to, the *Sachverhalt* is being constituted, the act is directed to, in the strict sense, the *object-about-which*. In the reflective, critical, act, the proposition, the *Sachverhalt as supposed*, becomes objectified. In the act of confirmation, when the judgment is validated, the *Sachverhalt* itself comes to self-givenness. Again, Husserl's position is not very far from Frege's. Not having the notion of higher-order constituted objectivities, Frege could only talk about the thought and of the true thought as being the fact. Having simplified his ontology by the doctrine of truth values, he was not in need of the "situation" (*Sachlage*) which makes both 'A > B' and 'B < A' true.

III

As I have said, Husserl and Frege held very similar views about names other than ordinary proper names. How are their views about ordinary proper names related? While Frege did want to extend the sense-reference distinction to ordinary proper names exactly as it applies to definite descriptions, he recognized that there was a special problem in this case. In a much-discussed footnote in "Sense and Reference," he writes:

> In the case of an actual proper name such as 'Aristotle' opinions as to sense may differ. It might, for instance, be taken to be the following: the pupil of Plato and teacher of Alexander the Great. Anybody who does this will attach another sense to the sentence 'Aristotle was born in Stagira" than will a man who takes as the sense of the name: the teacher of Alexander the Great who was born in Stagira. So long as the thing meant remains the same, such variations of sense may be tolerated, although they are to be avoided in the theoretical structure of a demonstrative science and ought not to occur in a perfect language.[30]

One point appears to be clear. For Frege, the variations in sense should not occur in an ideal language. As Dummett notes, the fact that Frege's model is not satisfied in actual linguistic practice, the model namely of one name—one sense, does not destroy the utility of that model; on the contrary, the model is "the only possible theory of the mechanism by which a name could acquire reference."

But while this in general is correct, such an understanding of Frege's position overlooks the nature of the shift from the period of the *Begriffsschrift* to that of "On Sense and Reference." To my knowledge, this point is best brought out by Hans Sluga.[31] In the *Begriffsschrift*, 'the mode of determination', Sluga points out, is a property of the signs, so that the way in which an object is given is to be reflected in the signs themselves. In the account of 1892, 'the mode of determination' is contained in the sense, but not necessarily reflected in the sign. Sluga concludes that as a consequence Frege allows that the name 'Aristotle' may well have many differ-

ent senses depending upon how, for a speaker, the object is determined. The *Begriffsschrift* was obviously concerned with an ideal
logical script. For Sluga, the shift may be understood as a change
from a Lotze-Leibniz account to a Kantian one.

On this interpretation, it is *not* the case that a proper name such
as 'Aristotle' *itself* is associated with an unambiguous sense and
with no other. If it were so, only then one could further maintain
that even if different persona did attach different senses to 'Aristotle,' in a perfect language only that sense which really belongs to
it will be assigned to the name, to the exclusion of all the others.
But which one of the descriptions gives the true sense, the sense
which will survive in the perfect language? How to single out this
sense from all the many possible true descriptions of Aristotle?

Two responses to this question are possible. 1) One may answer,
following Dummett, that the sense of a name need not be (in fact,
cannot be) a description.[32] Two reasons are offered for this interpretation of Frege. In the first place, none of the descriptions ('The
teacher of Alexander the Great', 'the most famous student of
Plato', etc.) could give the sense of 'Aristotle', for then one of the
many propositions 'Aristotle is the Φ', where 'the Φ' is a true description of the man, would have to be analytic. It is not obvious
that any one of these is analytic. The other reason adduced against
saying "the sense of 'Aristotle' is the same as the sense of 'the Φ'"
is that if the sense contains 'the mode of presentation', a proper
name and a description could not possibly have the same sense, for
they certainly present their objects differently.[33] On this interpretation, then, in saying that Aristotle is the Φ, one says what the
reference is, and while *saying* what the reference is, one *shows* the
sense. What the sense is cannot be directly stated, except trivially
by an expression such as "the sense of 'A'."[34]

Now, the contention that the sense of a proper name cannot in
principle be given by a description has to take into account two
objections. First, Frege himself, in the footnote quoted, gives descriptions, as examples of possible senses of 'Aristotle'. Second, the
sense of a proper name, in fact the sense of any name, becomes
something ineffable which can only be shown but not said (except
trivially by an expression of the sort "the sense of . . ."). Dummett
answers both these objections, but not to our complete satisfaction. His answer to the first objection is that when Frege gives
examples of possible senses by means of definite descriptions, "this

should be considered as merely a device for a brief characterization of a sense, rather than as a means of conveying the thesis which Kripke ascribes to Frege"—the thesis, namely, that for Frege the sense of a proper name is a definite description or a set of them.[35] The point being made by Dummett is obscure, for the distinction between "a brief characterization of a sense" and saying what the sense is, is left obscure. The only Fregean explication of that distinction could be in terms of the sense itself and the sense of that sense. But this is obviously what Dummett does not intend to mean in the present case. What he does appear to mean by the sense itself (rather than its brief characterization in a descriptive phrase) is "an associated criterion for recognizing a given object as the referent," a criterion which sometimes can, but sometimes cannot be, expressed by a definite description. Frege nowhere talks of "criteria" (Sluga considers this talk more Geach than Frege). To say that the sense of a name contains a specification of the sort of object the referent is,[36] is to say that it is part of the sense of 'Aristotle' that Aristotle is a man and also the sort of human he is. We are back with some version of the definite description theory.

To the objection that the interpretation leads to an ineffability thesis, Dummett replies that to master the sense is to determine the truth conditions, so that even if we cannot say what a sense is, we can say what someone can do when he grasps that sense.[37] Of course, one who grasps the sense knows what sort of object the expression under consideration refers to. There is therefore an objective test of whether one has correctly grasped the sense or not. In fact, there is nothing wrong in conceding a limited ineffability thesis, the thesis namely that the sense is *shown* in the very same act in which the referent is being talked about. But to rule out the possibility of a linguistic expression of this sense would make the theory of sense much less useful. If a linguistic expression of the sense is permitted, then what other form can it take, in the case of a proper name, excepting a definite description? But, then we are back at the familiar problem: which of the many true descriptions is the real sense of 'Aristotle'? Here we come to the second of the two responses.

2) Instead of saying that the sense of 'Aristotle' is not at all expressible in definite description, one may want to say that since the sense after all contains the mode of presentation, what sense one attaches to the proper name depends upon how the person

Aristotle is presented to one, the speaker or the hearer. Frege was right in emphasizing that different persons may attach different senses to 'Aristotle', for after all Aristotle may be "presented to," "thought of," referred to, in different manners, from different perspectives. This brings Frege nearer Husserl: meanings are conferred by intentional acts. They do not originally belong to signs. Signs derive their meanings from the interpretive acts of the speaker or the hearer, or of a community. To ask, then, what is *the sense* of 'Aristotle' would appear to be misconceived. To ask, what is the essence of Aristotle—a different question altogether—makes sense. The sense of 'Aristotle' and the essence of Aristotle need not coincide. Husserl was not altogether free from this confusion, although his theory had the potentiality of avoiding it.

I now turn to Husserl's views about the sense of an ordinary proper name such as 'Aristotle'. From all the scattered discussions in his works,[38] Husserl seems to be holding the following views: a proper name such as 'Aristotle' names directly, not attributely. "Directly" here means "without conceptual mediation." Thus, in the case of the indexical "this," there is a minimal conceptual mediation, "the thought of a pointing." In the case of 'Aristotle' even this much mediation is absent. Note that with this Husserl is reversing a position, widely held since Bertrand Russell, to the effect that 'this', rather than 'Aristotle', is more strictly a proper name. But to say that 'Aristotle' directly names should not be construed to mean that it is a mere index.[39] One difference between an index and a proper name is that while an index, by its essence, points to an existent reality, a name does not necessarily name what is. Nor is 'naming' the same as 'being a mark of', as Mill would have it. Naming is a sort of referring, the name is an expression, not a meaningless sign. Hence the name, even 'Aristotle,' has a *sense*. This sense, the 'proper meaning' as Husserl often calls it, is not to be construed as an attribute possessed by Aristotle, or a description true of him. If it were, then the sense of 'Aristotle' would have been something like that of "the most famous student of Plato." But a simple meaning like that of 'Aristotle', a meaning intended inarticulately, *in one ray*, as it were, could not be the same as meaning of an articulate, descriptive phrase, which is constituted step by step *in many rays*, as it were ['E is a, the Ea is b, the Eab is c, . . . ']. Saying "The capital of India *is called* New Delhi" makes use of the concept of "being called"; but the "individual, simple meaning" of 'New Delhi' is not "the capital of India." While the proper name directly names its object in such a manner, that the name is given as "a fixed appellation" of the thing (the man is known *as* Hans, the city *is* New Delhi, and so on), this simplicity of the meaning is to be contrasted with the complexity of the process in which our consciousness of the meaning may develop. One may articulate the sense through progressive predicative characterizations, but in that case one has new meanings which were not just implicitly there in the original inarticulate sense. But, even the simple 'proper meaning' of 'Aristotle' has a generality of its own, it succeeds in referring to Aristotle in the midst of varying 'presentations' of the man. This generality, however, is not that of a general name such as 'man'.

It is obvious that Husserl wants to take care of the major salient aspects of the situation: a proper name such as 'Aristotle' directly names and not attributely. Yet it has a *sense*, the object is presented in a certain manner. The sense however should be such that it permits "direct" naming, as opposed to mediated reference. Being inarticulate, the sense must be *simple*; articulate and specify it, and you have *new senses* which attributively refer. It is the same tension between the inarticulate sense and the articulate description which we encountered in the case of Frege's theory. In the *Ideas*, Husserl explicitly thematizes it as the distinction between prelinguistic, preconceptual *sense* and the conceptual *meaning*[40] (between what he there calls *Sinn* and *Bedeutung*).

IV

Indexicals present serious problems for both Frege and Husserl. For both, these expressions threaten their theories of objective and essentially communicable sense. Husserl refers to indexicals and their like as threatening "to plunge all our hard-won distinctions back into confusion."[41] These are what he calls *"essentially occasional"* expressions; in their case "it is essential to orient actual meaning to the occasion, the speaker and the situation."[42] How to reconcile these expressions (and their senses) with the theory that meaning is an ideal objective unity existing independently of the user's intentions and situations? Again let us begin with Frege.

Frege's discussion of indexicals is brief but pointed. It occurs in "Der Gedanke." After saying that sometimes the contents of a sentence go beyond the thoughts expressed by it (so that the thought is, in such cases, only a part of the content), Frege turns to those cases where the mere wording is not adequate to express the thought. In many of these cases, for example in the use of 'today' and 'yesterday', the *written* wording is not the complete expression of thought. To grasp the thought, knowledge of the circumstances accompanying the utterance is needed. Frege does not note, as Husserl does, that an actual *dialogical* situation contains "sufficiently reliable clues to guide the hearer to the meaning intended," that in such cases as well as in the case of 'here', 'now', 'I', and 'this', what the meaning is "can be gleaned only from the *living* utterance and from the *intuitive* circumstances which surround it."[43]

It would have been to the advantage of their theories if Frege and Husserl had held that indexicals denote, refer, but do not express any sense. But neither ever chose this way out. Not Frege, for if the sentence "I am in pain" is to express a thought, such thought can consist only of the senses of the component parts of the sentence. A thought cannot have as one or more of its components a referent. 'I' therefore must express a sense. Not Husserl, for he insisted that even when the hearer does not know who the speaker is, i.e., has no access to the speaker and so does not know the referent of 'I', he still, upon hearing the utterance "I am in pain," *understands* its meaning. What he grasps in so understanding, then, could not consist in identifying *who* is in pain. Even the word 'I' must have a sense, as distinguished from its reference.

But does the word 'I' have the same sense when uttered by different persons? Frege certainly held the view that a sentence containing the word 'I' expresses different thoughts when uttered by different people. Everyone is originally given to himself in a special and unique manner in which he cannot be given to anyone else. When Dr. Lauben thinks "I am injured," Frege writes, he will probably be "using" his own unique mode of self-presentation. The specific thought as determined by this unique mode of self-presentation can be apprehended only by Dr. Lauben himself. How then does he communicate it to the others? In order to be able to communicate, he must be using 'I' in a sense that is graspable by the others, e.g., in the sense "he who, at this moment, is speaking to you." But the thought that is thus communicable is most probably not the same as the thought Dr. Lauben himself grasps. Frege is thus led to a theory of incommunicable sense, which conflicts with his original theory of meaning.

That the *sense* of an indexical such as 'I' is not the same as its (linguistic) meaning has been recently emphasized by writers on Frege such as Tyler Burge.[44] Of course, when the word 'I' is uttered by different persons, its referent is different in each case. Its linguistic meaning, however, remains the same: this is the part of its meaning that is grasped by the hearer. But the sense, so far as it contains the mode of givenness, the epistemological perspective, varies from speaker to speaker.[45] The case with 'I' is different from ordinary proper names. Although different speakers may attach different senses to 'Aristotle', any such sense, once it is linguistically articulated, can be communicated and grasped.[46] But the unique sense which a speaker attaches to 'I' is incommunicable. It may not even be conceptually and linguistically articulable.[47] The theory therefore offers a two-tiered structure: a communicable basic stratum and an incommunicable stratum. Perry calls the former the "role," that which according to him carries us from the occasion to the object. The role (= linguistic meaning) of an indexical is unchanging, the object (or, value, as Perry calls it) changes from context to context. The role is to be distinguished from the Fregean sense: while the role takes us from the context to the object, the Fregean sense, Perry insists, is meant to take us directly to the object. Such a sense, if there is any, would be private and incommunicable.

A similar two-tiered theory is to be found in Husserl. He distinguishes between "the universal semantic function"[48] of an indexical and what it means in any specific case. The specific meaning, in each case, is determined by the context of utterance, in the case of 'I' by the utterer, in the case of 'this' by perception.[49] The universal meaning, which Husserl also calls the *"anzeigende Bedeutung"*—the same as Perry's "role"—remains unchanging from context to context, while the specific sense, the *"angezeigte Bedeutung,"* varies with context, utterer, and perceptual orientation. Not unlike Frege, Husserl would rather eliminate such fluctuations from scientific discourse, but both are forced to recognize their recalcitrant character for their theories and indispensability for natural languages.

There is, however, an important difference in their approaches to the entire problem. They share a common problem: namely, how to accommodate the context-dependence and fluctuating character of the senses of indexicals within a theory of objective, self-subsistent, ideal meanings? Frege could only say that we have to recognize some kinds of senses which are incommunicable. Did Husserl recognize such incommunicable senses? I think Husserl's phenomenological orientation forces him to look at the same situation from a somewhat different perspective. "Since we regularly understand such expressions in normal circumstances, the very idea of these circumstances, and of their regular relation to the expression, involves the presence of generally graspable, sufficiently reliable clues to guide the hearer to the meaning intended in the case in question."[50] I think Husserl's problem may be formulated thus: since we do grasp the sense intended by the speaker in an actual, living, dialogical situation, then such a situation must be able to provide the hearer with clues that lead him to supply what Perry calls "completing" sense; therefore what we need to understand is how such clues operate. Frege's point seems to be that thought expressed by a sentence containing 'I' is in fact never graspable by anyone other than the speaker. Husserl's problem is transcendental: since we do understand the other when he says "I am wounded," there must be some way of making up for the lack, for the fact that the hearer cannot have the speaker's self-presentation. Before I proceed to explore what Husserl has to say by way of specifying what these transcendental conditions of understanding are, one more question needs to be dealt with.

The question is, how can something be a Fregean *sense* and yet be incommunicable? It may be true that, as Frege writes, "everyone is presented to himself in a particular and primitive way, in which he is presented to no one else."[51] Or as Husserl writes, "Each man has his own I-presentation (and with it his individual notion of I)" and the word 'I' "has not itself directly the power to arouse the specific I-presentation,"[52] it is still arguable that this specific I-presentation is a *Vorstellung* and *not* a sense. In order to be an incommunicable sense, it must first of all be a sense. Since *Vorstellungen* are in any case incommunicable, the thesis that there is an incommunicable I-presentation can only be significant if this I-presentation amounts to a sense and is not a *Vorstellung*. In what sense, then, is it a sense? If this I-presentation is such that it consists in a set of predicates, a description, that I alone know to be true of myself (I, e.g., know myself to be such and such a person), then there is no reason why I cannot let others know what I take myself to be. *In principle*, at least, such a sense could not be incommunicable. (Note that the predicates need not be true of me, it is enough if I take them to be true.) On the other hand, there may be, and in fact are, changing perceptions that I may have of myself, depending on circumstances such as health or sickness, success or failure, which one may not want to count as modes of *self*-givenness in the sense in which such a mode is contained in the sense of 'I' for myself. In between these extremes—the availability of a descriptive account (in which case, we have a Fregean sense but not, in principle, incommunicability) and the varying modes of self-presentation dependent on circumstances in which I find myself (in which case, we have incommunicability but not a sense, but possibly a self-*feeling*)—we have to look for the incommunicable *sense* of 'I'. Could it be unvarying mode of self-understanding, a self-interpretation which cannot be fully conceptualized, but which remains for me a constant accompaniment of every use of 'I' on my part? If there is such an unvarying, non-conceptual, inarticulate self-*understanding*, then that precisely could be a sense, without being communicable. Husserl perhaps was thinking of some such notion of 'I', when he added within parentheses in the text quoted above, "and with it his individual notion of I." (One should not confuse with this what has been called an "individual concept" which is, for some, the sense of ordinary proper names such as 'Aristotle'. The question is not, if there is such a concept that is true only of Aristotle and of none else, or in our present case, true of me and of none else. The question is, what sense I attach to 'Aristotle' and take to be true of him, and to 'I' and take to be true of me alone.)

Although we still do not know for certain what this incommunicable sense is, we know *where* to look for it. We are again faced with the idea of a preconceptual sense, an idea we had to confront while discussing the case of ordinary proper names as well. There, the preconceptual, perceptual sense of 'Aristotle' permits conceptualization (possibly in terms of Aristotle's physiognomy); here, it appears to exclude that possibility.

Let us now return to Husserl's account of *how* communication is nevertheless possible. To begin with, although *indexicals* have the two layers of sense referred to earlier, Husserl adds that whereas for the speaker the two layers are presented together, in fact, are not distinguished from one another, for the hearer they are presented in a sequence: first, "an indefinitely referential idea," then the full authentic meaning. In moving from the one to the other, the hearer has to depend upon the "reliable clues" provided by *an already familiar* world. In the *Formal and Transcendental Logic*, where discussion of this theme receives a new orientation, "the vast realm of *occasional judgments*" is said to owe its intersubjective truth or falsity to "the relatedness of the single subject's and the community's whole daily life to a typical specific likeness among situations."[53] Any such situation has "situational horizons," which, in Husserl's new vocabulary, is an accomplishment of the "constituting horizon-intentionality." We are then told that it is this horizon-intentionality which *"essentially determines the sense of occasional judgments*—always, and far beyond what at any time is, or can be, said expressly and determinately in the words themselves." In a footnote to this sentence, Husserl writes: "In the *Logische Untersuchungen*, I still lacked the theory of horizon-intentionality, the all-determining role of which was first brought out in the *Ideen*. Therefore, in the earlier work, I could not finish with occasional judgments and their signification."[54]

Without undertaking to expound Husserl's transcendental constitutive phenomenology, the point he is making here may be restated thus: the idea of horizon-intentionality breaks open the bounds of the previously conceived (Cartesian) egological consciousness, thereby making possible a world of familiar and typical situations shared in common. In the dialogical situation, it is this typicality which makes it possible for the hearer to provide the "completing sense." Written text lacks this aid. Frege recognizes this difference between written text and living speech: "If such a sentence is written down, it often no longer has a complete sense because there is nothing to indicate who uttered it, and where and when."[55]

V

Most of the differences between Husserl and Frege that I have been drawing attention to may be traced to one deep, underlying difference. I want to express this difference thus:

For Husserl, the meanings are meanings of *acts*, for Frege, they are meanings of *signs*.

(1) The first half of this thesis will not be challenged by anyone who knows Husserl's texts. I will quote only one text in support. At the very beginning of the Sixth Logical Investigation, we find the following sentence: "The expressive role in speech lies, accordingly, not in mere words, but in expressive acts."[56] The expressive role here is that of expressing meanings. The First Logical Investigation is entitled "Expression and Meaning." In fact, Husserl is concerned with the acts which transform a bare sign into a meaningful expression. The *act of utterance* or producing a physical sound is first made one, he tells us,[57] with the *meaning-intention*, and when the relation of the expression to its object is *realized*, as when we say "red" while seeing a red color. The meaning-intention, in its turn, is made one with its corresponding *fulfillment*. Thus the three acts enter into an intimately fused unity. In the hearer, the function of the word is to awaken a sense-conferring act and to guide interest in the direction of fulfillment of the intention.[58] Each of these acts has its logical content: the word as such, the meaning as such, and the *fulfilling sense*. It is such a fusion of acts which explains, for Husserl, how, as he puts it in the Sixth Investigation,[59] "the name 'my inkpot' seems to *overlay* the perceived object, to belong sensibly to it. . . . Not word *and* inkpot; but the act-experiences . . . in which they make their appearance, are here brought into relation." As a consequence, the expression seems "to clothe the object like a garment."[60]

I think the thesis that Husserlian meanings are meanings *of* acts is true not only of the early theory of the First Logical Investigation, but also of the later theory of *Noema*. For the earlier version, meanings are species of which particular acts intending them are instantiations; according to the later version, meanings are (intentional) correlates of acts. The versions differ as to how to understand the relation between an act and its meaning, but both accept that meanings are meanings *of* acts.[61]

Both the noema and the Fregean *Sinne* are *abstract* entities in that, as emphasized by Føllesdal, they cannot be sensually perceived. But the noema is, while the Fregean *Sinn* is not, abstract in another sense (in a sense of 'abstract', often used by Husserl): the noema is inseparable from an act, the noema and act constitute one *concrete* structure. The noema cannot *be* by itself, save as component (not a real part, but an intentional correlate) of an act. This point, in my view, is often missed by interpreters of Husserl, who place one-sided emphasis on noematic phenomenology. (The noetic phenomenologists commit the opposite error.) In section 98 of *Ideas* I, "Mode of Being of the Noema," Husserl writes that the noema is an entity that is "wholly dependent. . . . Its *esse* consists exclusively in its *percipi*, except that the meaning of this statement is about as far removed as it can be from that of Berkeley, since here the *percipi* does not contain the *esse* as a real (*reelles*) constituent." Eidetically speaking, "the Eidos of the noema points to the Eidos of the noetic consciousness; both belong *eidetically* together."

What about the following text from *Ideas* I, section 124: "Logical meaning is an expression. . . . Whatever is 'meant as such', every meaning in the noematic sense (indeed as noematic nucleus) or any act whatsoever can be expressed through logical meanings." This text does not mean that every noema is linguistic, but only that it *can be* linguistically expressed, *with suitable adjustments*. As I like to put it, the act of expressing, among all intentional acts, has the privileged status that in it the entire life of intentional consciousness can be mapped onto itself.

(2) The second half of my thesis, namely, that for Frege senses are senses of signs, may indeed prove controversial. It may be challenged on two grounds. In the first place, it will be pointed out, Frege did concern himself, especially in his later works, with acts. Secondly, it will be said, the Fregean senses are not linguistic meanings, but cognitive contents. It is true that in the *Logische Untersuchungen*, especially in "Der Gedanke" and "Verneinung," Frege shows interest in mental acts such as thinking, judging asserting, and denying. But it must be said that the senses remain *externally* related to such acts, and there is no suggestion of a concept of intentionality of these acts. The senses are still senses of the appropriate signs. The mental acts grasp them, or take up some appropriate attitude toward them. Tyler Burge, in his excellent paper "Sinning against Frege,"[62] has convincingly argued that the Fregean *Sinne* are not linguistic meanings and that it would be misleading to render "Gedanke" as "proposition" if "proposition" is understood after the linguistic philosophers. If the concept of 'sense' was introduced by Frege to account for 'cognitive value', sense must have something to do with our cognitive acts, with beliefs, for example. Burge sometimes characterizes them as cog-

nitive contents. But at the same time, he recognizes that they are also eternally existing thoughts which one grasps. The decisive question, then, is: how can a thought be both an eternally existing structure *and* a cognitive content of a real mental act? I think Frege's use of 'Inhalt', where he does use it to characterize the senses, should be construed as meaning 'object'. When in our act of thinking I grasp a thought, the thought is not the *content* but the *object* of my grasping. Frege's philosophy of mind, with his *strong* notion of subjectivity, cannot have room for any idea of content other than the purely private, incommunicable, subjective experiences, which the senses are far from being. That in an act one grasps an object does not, by itself, amount to the thesis of intentionality. One needs some concept of structure *of* the act (and not merely a structure which that act grasps) which would account for its directedness. This requires that two acts of grasping two different senses would still be different, qua acts, by their internal structures, and not merely by virtue of their having different objects. G. E. Moore held the view that sensing of blue and sensing of yellow, qua sensing, are identical and that they differ only insofar as blue differs from yellow. This concept of sensing is not yet an intentional concept. Frege's concept of grasping is equally nonintentional. Since the senses are abstract entities, Frege encountered the problems associated with *intensionality,* but he did not arrive at a concept of *intentionality.* If then by 'linguistic meaning' one means either a set of synonymous linguistic expressions, or rules of using the expression concerned, Frege's senses are not linguistic meanings. In this I agree with Burge. But if by 'linguistic meaning' is meant the meaning *of* a linguistic sign, Frege's *sense* appears to me to be linguistic meaning. The eternally existing thoughts are *senses only insofar as* they are *associated* with expressions of a language.

Against the contention that the Fregean senses are not *of* acts, the following objection may be raised. One reason why the concept of sense is introduced is that it helps to account for the fact that one and the same object may be presented under different descriptions, or grasped as ϕ in one act and as ψ in another. Now, if Frege's senses can do that, then what more is needed—it may be asked— to make them senses of the appropriate acts? To put the matter differently: let an act α grasp an object o *as* ϕ, and another act β grasp the same object o *as* ψ. What more is needed, then, in order to justify the statement that ϕ is the sense of the act α and ψ is the sense of the act β? This, however, is not Frege's point. Were it so, Frege's and Husserl's concepts of sense would have been the same. Of course, an act of presenting the planet Venus as the morning star does grasp Venus as the morning star. But it is not the act of presentation which originarily—for Frege—does this. It is the expression "morning star" which, through *its* sense, refers to Venus *as* the morning star. The mental act of thinking of Venus as the morning star is not only not constitutive of that sense, but is itself possible because the expression "morning star" has that sense and that reference in the first place. Likewise in judging. A sentence itself expresses a *thought*, while an act of judging consists in *grasping* that thought and recognizing its truth value.

For my present purposes, it will be best not to take up the rather controversial question of whether Frege is to be counted as a linguistic philosopher. However, I will, at this point, recall what Dummett has recently characterized as the central issue in that controversy.[63] Granted that the senses are timeless entities, it still remains to be asked, how does one come to associate a sense with a word or a sentence? In what does our attaching a sense to a word consist? If it is an inner mental connection, then what happens is that when the speaker (or the hearer) hears the word, that sense comes to his mind. According to Dummett, such an answer would be opposed to Frege's theory of sense. "A sense is not a mental content, like an idea (*Vorstellung*) or an image," Dummett writes, "there is no such process as a sense's coming into the mind."[64] Furthermore, Dummett takes such an account to be inconsistent with Frege's anti-psychologism, for it makes senses subjective. Thirdly, on the associationist account (which is how Dummett understands the above theory of "inner mental connection"), the hearer can never be sure that the speaker associates the same sense with the word as the speaker does. In all this, Dummett is assuming that an interpretation of Frege as *not* being a linguistic philosopher requires that prior to or independently of acquiring a language, one grasps the senses and *then* subsequently treats a word as the bearer of a sense. If this is the case, then one needs an account of the mechanism by which the word acquires that sense, and *also*—note that this is a different issue than the preceding one—an account of how the hearer rightly understands the speaker, i.e., associates the same sense with the same word as the speaker does.

What is required is not that one *always* correctly understands what the other means, but that it should be possible, in principle, to compare one's sense with the other's and to say whether they are the same or not. Both on the psychologistic theory (that sense = mental content) and the associationist account of connection between words and their (objective) senses, such comparison is not possible. According to Dummett, even if the senses themselves be objective, if their connection with words is mental we would be back in the same situation as with a psychologism which identifies senses with mental entities. We would have, in effect, taken back what we had achieved.

Dummett's own interpretation of Frege on this point consists of two theses. In the first place, "to grasp the sense of a word is to comprehend its contribution to fixing the condition for any sentence containing it to be true."[65] Secondly, and this, for Dummett, follows from the first, "what a speaker takes the truth-condition of a sentence to be is manifested by the use he makes of that sentence and of others containing words occurring in it."[66] From both, he draws the conclusion that "the sense which a speaker attaches to a sentence must be ascertainable from his observable behavior, from what he says and does." He concedes that although the first thesis is explicitly there in Frege, the second is not to be found in his writings, and yet only such an interpretation can save him from losing all the gains made from rejecting psychologism and can account for the communicability of thoughts. In spite of his admission that senses are eternally existing entities, then, Frege remains a linguistic philosopher. *Our* only access to senses is through the linguistic expressions, even if the idea of beings who grasp the same thoughts as we do, without grasping them as senses of linguistic expressions, is regarded by him as consistent. (Compare Kant's view that although *we* can intuit only through sensibility, the idea of an intellectual intuition is consistent.)

It cannot be denied that our only access to senses is through their linguistic expressions. However, in order to get a total picture of the situation, one needs to keep in mind, along with this, not only the fact (of which Dummett is fully aware) that the idea of a nonlinguistic grasp of a sense is consistent, but also several other facts. In the first place, in oblique speech and intensional contexts, a sense is an object of reference as much as other objects are in straightforward speech: as object of reference, it is as little linguistic as are any other sorts of objects that may be referred to. Nevertheless, it may be argued, this is not a very significant point, for after all the primary mode of givenness of a sense qua sense is through the linguistic expression which expresses it (not through that which refers to it). To mitigate therefore the strength of the claim that the senses are linguistic entities, it needs to be pointed out that even when they are grasped through linguistic means, the idea of grasping implies that what is being grasped is not itself linguistic (in the same way as consciousness of an object implies that the object of the consciousness is distinct from the consciousness of that object). What is more, many different linguistic expressions, not alone in the same language but belonging to different languages, express the same sense, and so may provide access to it, from which it appears to follow that the sense itself is not *intrinsically* related to any language in particular. Both Frege and Husserl feel forced to recognize that there not only are unexpressed senses (of which therefore we are unaware), but that the phenomenon of new concepts (correlatively, new vocabulary) being formed suggests the emergence of some of these hitherto unexpressed senses from their anonymity into the reaches of human minds. Lastly, the not uncommon experience that available expressions are not adequate for the purpose of conveying a sense already at our disposal, suggests that a nonlinguistic availability of senses is always on the horizon of our more common linguistic commerce with them.

All or most of these may be conceded by the linguistic philosopher. He may still ask, how does a sense get attached to a linguistic expression? If the sense is not a *Vorstellung*, then an associationist account must be rejected. Frege recognizes that the mode of connection of a sense with its sign must be very different from the mode of connection of a *Vorstellung* with the sign that "associatively" evokes it. However, the only alternative to the associationist account is not the account offered by the linguistic philosopher who ties a sense, not to a given sign associatively, but to the use that one makes of that sign, word, or sentence. It is one thing to say that the hearer comes to understand what the speaker means by observing the use he makes of the linguistic expressions. It is another to say that the senses which the speaker grasps, or the hearer assigns to the utterances of the speaker, are *in fact* attached to the appropriate uses. For, then, one can raise the same question over again: how does a use come to manifest a certain sense?

The difficulties that suggest a linguistic formulation such as Dummett's derive from the fact that Frege assigns senses to signs with which they have no intrinsic relation, as also from the fact that he has an inadequate concept of mental acts which is unable to bear the burden of intersubjective availability of senses, should it be held that the senses originally attach to the acts. Husserl's account offers a third possibility, other than associationistic psychologism and linguistic theory. According to this account, senses originally belong to mental acts, not as real, private components, but as their ideal correlates. Mental acts *insofar as* they intend such senses are linguistically expressible.[67] The senses, being ideal objectivities, are *in principle* available for intersubjective sharing and communication. How *in a particular case* the hearer understands the speaker depends upon "reliable clues" which both publicly observable behavior (including linguistic use) and the familiar typicalities of the situations and contexts of discourse provide. There is no certainty that communication may not fail. But the life world has sufficient typicalities and the mental acts have sufficient numbers of eidetic structures to allow for enough communicability to begin with.

VI

Attempts to appropriate Husserl to Frege have led to a supposedly new interpretation of the concept of *noema*. This "new" interpretation, first succinctly formulated by Dagfinn Føllesdal,[68] understands the Husserlian noema as an intensional entity, as a generalization of the notion of meaning. I do not think this by itself goes against the standard interpretations. It appears as though what Husserl does is to generalize the concept of meaning of linguistic expressions over the field of all acts, so that the noema would still be a linguistic meaning. In fact, however, even in the First Logical Investigation, meaning, for Husserl, is meaning of expressive *acts*, not of the mere sign. Consequently, it is the concept of meaning of linguistic *acts*, that is generalized to the field of all *acts*. Of the eleven propositions about 'noema' which Føllesdal puts together, only the first, eighth, ninth, and tenth can be used to justify the claim to novelty of the interpretation. That the noema has a component which is common to all acts that have the same object with exactly the same properties, oriented in the same manner, and a component corresponding to the thetic character of the act; that the act relates to its object by virtue of its noema; that the noema of an act is not its object; that for one and the same noema there is only one corresponding object, while for one and the same object there may be several different corresponding noemata; further, that several different noematic *Sinne* may correspond to one and the same object and that each act has one and only one noema—all these are fairly well agreed upon by interpreters of Husserl. The new Fregean interpretation, as contrasted with the traditional understanding, holds in addition to these that the noema is an *abstract entity*, that it cannot be sensually perceived, and that it is known only through a special sort of reflection called the phenomenological reflection. (Note that although the Fregean sense is an abstract entity, atemporal and supersensible, grasping a sense does not involve performing any special sort of reflection. In every act of understanding, we grasp the appropriate senses. Of course, Frege did hold that a sense becomes the object of *reference* in oblique speech and in intensional contexts, but when we understand direct speech, we also do *grasp* the senses. Frege had no use of a special sort of reflection for thematizing them. Although the senses do not have names in ordinary language, such an expression as "the sense of 'x'" may be said to refer to, and so name a sense.)

Let me now turn to the views of Aron Gurwitsch (with which Føllesdal's interpretation of noema is generally contrasted). According to Gurwitsch, the noema is an ideal, atemporal, entity "which belongs to the same sphere as meanings or significations,"[69] a *sense* which may correspond to an indefinite number of acts.[70] Thus far, there is no difference between the standard, Gurwitsch view and the new interpretation. The difference pertains, not to noema in general, but to perceptual noema, and the decisive question with regard to the perceptual noema is: is it a *percept*, or an abstract entity? As and when I am perceiving an object, am I also, in some sense, experiencing, perhaps even perceiving, the noema of that perceptual act? Is the perceptual noema *given* to the percipient in that very act whose noema it is? Or, should we rather say that the perceptual noema, like all noemata, is a supersensible, abstract entity, which, while making possible, perceptual intentionality, itself remains imperceptible, but can be thematized only in a subsequent act of reflection?

Gurwitsch speaks of the perceptual noema as the perceived *as such*,[71] as being "the object just (exactly so and only so) as the perceiving subject is aware of it,"[72] "the object just, exactly just, as the subject has it in view."[73] There are also passages where the perceived *as such* is identified with the thing just as it appears, also with the perceptual adumbration, *the manners of appearance and presentation,*[74] "the perceptual appearance,"[75] and—shall we also say with Dreyfus? —with a perspectival view and a look?[76] If the noema is the appearance, the look, the view, then it makes sense to say that whenever I perceive an object, I *also experience* a noema. If, then, Gurwitsch's 'perceptual noema' (and Husserl's, in his view) is the percept, the object as perceived (as contradistinguished from the object which is perceived), then Dreyfus's point against it is well taken. For, then, the noema is no longer an ideal meaning (for how can a perceptual appearance, a look, a view, be an ideal entity?) and the distinction between the noema and the object will stand obliterated (for the noema would be *the object* exactly as it is being perceived). Of course, Gurwitsch holds the view (which admittedly is his revision of Husserl's) that the object is *nothing but* a noematic system, which on its part looks like obliterating that distinction. But this latter thesis is not what we are presently concerned with. We are trying to understand the other thesis — namely, that the perceptual noema is the perceived *as such*. One can hold this thesis, but may not want to subscribe to the other one. But is Gurwitsch's perceptual noema a percept, a sense datum, an appearance, or something of that genre? Admittedly, some of his formulations are misleading in this regard, but let us also recall some of the other things he says about the perceptual noema. In the first place, the entire discourse about noemata, belonging as it does to transcendental phenomenology, presupposes the transcendental epoche. In the case of perception, we must have overcome the natural attitude, put within brackets belief in the existence of the object of perception, and, most importantly, for Gurwitsch, rejected the constancy hypothesis, before we are in a position to speak of the perceptual noema.[77] The perceptual noema could not therefore be the perceived object. In order to be able to isolate and thematize the perceived as such, it is not enough to thematize the sensory data, the given appearance, the look, or the view. The thesis about the perspectival character of outer perception, by itself, does not have the resources to yield the concept of perceptual noema; left to itself it will yield the concept of 'aspects' of the perceptual object. What we need is the thesis of perception being an intentional act (with the implied opacity) and also a performance of the epoche. The perceptual noema is not, therefore, the same as the percept either of the naturalistic psychologies or of a theory of perception worked out within the parameters of the naturalistic attitude.

Gurwitsch could not then be saying that as and when I perceive an object, I also perceive, or experience, the perceptual noema. The noema is *involved in* the perceptual situation, in some important sense making possible perceptual reference, but it is not itself being perceived or experienced. One needs to suspend the natural attitude, cease to posit the object qua a real object out there, put into brackets inherited prejudices such as the constancy hypothesis, in order to be able to lay bare the noema of the act. Even if the perceptual noema is the perceived as such, it is not the perceived. *The perceived as such is not the simply perceived.* Gurwitsch's many other characterizations of the perceptual noema support the reading that he does not want to take it as the percept. He writes, for example, that one noema contains others in the sense of referring to them.[78] Now no percept, or appearance, or look contains other such entities within itself. No datum, in fact, could have such intentional references, such potentialities and horizons within its structure. Gurwitsch also writes, "the total system of noemata is to be considered as the 'equivalent of consciousness' or the 'equivalent correlate' of the perceptual thing."[79]

I must conclude therefore that although the Gestalt-theoretic context of the discourse makes it appear as if the perceptual noema, on Gurwitsch's reading, is a percept, it is in fact an entity of a different sort; that the discourse about noemata is a different sort of discourse than the discourse about percepts and appearances. I would therefore suggest that the Gurwitschean perceptual noema is not a *sensible* phenomenon. It is "the equivalent of consciousness" or "equivalent correlate" of the perceived thing.[80] It is concrete inasmuch as it permits description of its components, but what one describes is not the thing out there, not a sense datum or an appearance in the visual or phenomenal space, but a structure of the consciousness, in this case of the act of perceiving. The noema is grasped then in phenomenological *reflection on* the "reduced" act, not with eyes or any of the other sense organs.

We are now left with two options. One may want to hold that in the case of perception, there is no Fregean sense, there is only the object, bodily present before the perceiver. Alternatively, one may want to say that even in perception, the sense is a Fregean abstract entity. The latter is Føllesdal's position. There is no doubt that the former is not Husserl's position, notwithstanding his emphasis on the bodily givenness of the object of perception.

In proposing the former, Dreyfus is especially concerned with perceptual acts which are fulfilling acts *par excellence*. One of his contentions is that Husserl's Fregean concept of sense, appropriate as it is for 'signitive' acts, cannot legitimately be applied to perceptual acts. In effect, Dreyfus is challenging the validity of Husserl's concept of 'fulfilling sense' or 'perceptual noema'. Thus, writes Dreyfus,

> in the First Logical Investigation acts were divided into signifying and fulfilling acts. Then the perceptual act, which one would suppose to be a fulfilling act par excellence, was in turn analyzed into *its* signifying and intuitive components. . . . Thus a regress develops in which sense coincides with sense indefinitely. At each stage we arrive at a fulfilling meaning for an intending meaning, but at no stage does the fulfilling meaning imply a sensuous filling.[81]

In other words, if part of the reason for the distinction between sense and reference lies in the fact that one may perform an act in which an object is 'emptily', merely 'signitively' intended, referred to as being such and such without such intention being fulfilled, without the object itself being bodily given, *then* to make the same distinction again in the case of perceptual acts would require that even in perception the object is not bodily presented, that the perceptual intention is in need of further fulfillment. But this would only contradict the very sense of perception which, by definition, presents its object bodily and directly. In Dreyfus's words the perceptual meaning has to be an 'incarnate meaning', an *Anschauungssinn*, and not an interpretative meaning, *Auffassungssinn* (which the Fregean *Sinn* has to be); it has to be "an entirely new sort of sense whose existence would be essentially inseparable from the intuitive content of the object whose sense it was."[82]

Dreyfus's criticism, if valid, would not only need a total revision of Husserl's philosophy of perception, but would also need a turning away from transcendental phenomenology to existential phenomenology. I will not comment on this latter claim. What I want to do is try to understand why it is that Husserl introduced the concept of 'fulfilling sense' or 'perceptual noema' when he explicitly recognized both the fulfilling character of perception and the necessary separation between the 'noema' and its 'filling'. In fact, it would seem that the notion of a fulfilling sense is a self-contradictory notion. What could have led Husserl to it?

Each particular perceptual act presents its object bodily; it is an experience of concrete 'filling'. No two acts of perceiving are identical. Each is, to say the least, numerically distinct. Also, no two acts of judging are identical. The same applies to other kinds of acts as well. However, one does speak of the same judgment, the same belief, the same doubt. One may also speak of the same perception. One may, in an important sense, say "I have now the same perception as you had then." In the *Logical Investigations*, Husserl sought to explicate this sense of 'sameness', to give a criterion of identity of acts. Two acts may be said to be identical, in this sense, when they have the same 'quality' and the same 'matter':

> Talk about the same presentation, judgment etc. points to no individual sameness of acts, as if my consciousness were in some way conjoined with someone else's. It also means no relation of perfect likeness, of indiscernibility as regards inner constituents, as if the one act merely duplicated the other.[83]

This unity of matter and quality is what Husserl calls the intentional essence of an act. He recognizes that the intentional essence does not exhaust the act phenomenologically.[84] If this concept of identity—Husserl in fact calls it a 'conceptual ruling'[85]—applies not merely to signitive acts but also to perception, then one can speak of the 'intentional essence' of a perceptual act. A perceptual act may then have the same 'matter' as another, however they may differ from one another otherwise. It is this concept of 'matter' which becomes the *Sinn* of the *Ideas*. It is thus that he arrives at the 'perceptual *Sinn*' or 'noema'.

We have to keep in mind two things. First, the perceptual sense does not contain the entire "fullness" (*Fülle*) of perceptual experience: "all differences of fulness which go beyond mere identification, and which variously determine peculiarities of fulfillment and increase of fulfillment, have no relevance in the formation of this conception."[86] Again: "the 'fulfilling sense' carries no implication of fulness, that it does not accordingly include the total content of the intuitive act, to the extent that this is relevant for the theory of knowledge."[87] Identity of percept in the above-defined sense is compatible with differences in the descriptive contents of the experiences. Second, the perceptual sense is not the same as the meaning of the corresponding linguistic expression. With regard to this last point, it is well known that Husserl recognized a close relation between the sense of an act and the meaning of the corresponding linguistic expression. But he also did not want to identify them. In section 124 of *Ideas* I, he lays down the thesis that the senses of all acts can be expressed conceptually through linguistic meanings. Husserl also points out that 'expression' indicates "a special act-stratum" to which all other acts must adjust themselves in their own way and with which they must blend remarkably in such wise that every noematic act-meaning, and consequently the relation to objectivity which lies in it, stamps itself "conceptually" in the noematic phase of the "expressing."[88] Making allowances for the inadequacies of the metaphors he uses here ("stamping," "copying," "mirroring"), we can say that the meaning of a perceptual statement like "This is white" is a conceptualization of the sense of the perceptual experience which that statement expresses. The perceptual sense, then, is not conceptual, the meaning of the perceptual statement is, and the two are not identical. Besides, in spite of a certain 'congruence' between the two, "the upper layer need not extend its expressing function over the entire lower layer."[89] Furthermore,

> The stratum of the meaning-function is not, and in principle is not, a sort of duplication of the lower stratum. Many directions of variability in the latter do not appear at all in the meaning whose function it is to express; they and their correlates do not 'express themselves' at all; so it is with the modifications of relative clearness and distinctness, the attentional modifications, and so forth.[90]

I have said that Husserl's 'Bedeutung' is not the same as Frege's 'Sinn'. Husserl's *Bedeutung* is the meaning of an *act* of expression, Frege's *Sinn* is the meaning of the expression as a physical object. Now, we may add that although Husserl's *Bedeutung* is ideal and conceptual (like Frege's *Sinn*), not all noemata for Husserl are conceptual. The Husserlian *Sinn* of nonlinguistic acts, though expressible (within limitations), is nonconceptual; and when it is "expressed," the meaning of the expression and the *Sinn* are 'congruent' but not identical. The *Sinn* or noema is always ideal. 'Ideality' and 'conceptuality' are not the same. Much of Dreyfus's criticism of Husserl's 'perceptual noema' rests upon an interpretation according to which all Husserlian *Sinne*, like the Fregean, are conceptual—which, as we have just seen, is not the case.

Let us now return to Dreyfus's main argument: namely, that the Husserlian concept of perceptual noema leads to an infinite regress, that perception is an immediate and direct encounter with its object. Dreyfus concedes that in the case of seeing *that*, there needs to be something like a Husserlian *Sinn*: seeing *that* . . . is not referentially transparent, it does not go direct to the object, it is mediated by conceptual meanings. Thus, Husserl writes: "*Mere* sense, however, never fulfils categorical acts, or intentions which include categorical forms: fulfilment [sic] lies rather, in every case, in a sensibility structured by categorical acts."[91]

The cases of direct seeing, as contradistinguished from cases of seeing that . . . , are referentially transparent and free from conceptual mediation; it is in these cases that the Husserlian—and Fregean—*Sinne* are, according to Dreyfus, uncalled-for. In order to be able to appreciate Husserl's position, let us recall the relevant aspects of Husserl's philosophy of perception. First, the thesis that perception is perspectival: this thesis requires that perceptual adumbrations point beyond themselves to other possible ones, so that although the overriding intention is nevertheless directed to the object perceived, the object as such is nothing but the "Idea of the completely fulfilled sense."[92] The dialectic of the presented and the appresented, which underlies the perceptual situation, is different from the distinction between the intuitively given and the emptily intended. The latter underlies the Fregean distinction between conceptual *Sinn* and reference; the former underlies Husserl's theory of perception. Within the total horizon of a fulfilling act (which fulfills a prior empty intention of the object now being perceived), there nevertheless are unfulfilled intentions which point toward further possibilities of fulfillment, further determinations of the "inner horizon" of the object. By abolishing this possibility, we can have a philosophy of perception in which the object is directly perceived all at once, so that perception achieves a satiety and points to nothing beyond it. But that would not be a phenomenologically satisfactory position.

Further, when an act of perceiving of mine fulfills a prior meaning intention, it is not every detail of the act, every *hic et nunc*, that plays that role or that is necessary for the total act's playing that role. It is not qua this act and qua mine that it plays the fulfilling role. Rather *any such* act (my perception at some other time as well as someone else's perception now) could have played the same role. Hence, within a fulfilling experience, one may single out a central core by virtue of which, alone, the act fulfills *that* intention and none other.

The same perception may serve to fulfill or verify different intentions (e.g., "This is white," "This is not red"). Here again, we need to recognize that the same perception's differing role requires a different 'slice' of its body to serve as its fulfilling sense.

It would seem then that Husserl's notion of perceptual noema is phenomenologically well founded, and the extension of *his* concept of meaning to perceptual acts is indeed a sound philosophical achievement. A theory of perception which dispenses with the noema and seeks to rehabilitate a direct realism has to fall back on the classical, not the Husserlian, transcendental consciousness. The counterpart of the purely objective is the pure transcendental consciousness. If human subjectivity, both in its bodily and its intellectual dimensions, is "condemned to meanings," as Merleau-Ponty says, it is not clear how, by replacing the noetic act by the bodily 'set', we can hope to get rid of the mediating '*Sinn*', when the body, phenomenologically considered, is not a physical object but an intentional movement. If the body is intentional, a bodily 'set' cannot logically guarantee real existence of that toward which it is directed, and the object would be *intended* by the bodily movement and there would always be a gap between the object as such and the object as intended.

Of the two alternatives proposed, then, the first is not Husserlian. The second, namely that perception is mediated by a *sense* which is a Fregean abstract entity, is Husserlian, *provided* one is not misled by the phrase "Fregean abstract entity." One component of this thesis is that the noema is an intensional entity. Another component is that the noema is not sensuously apprehended. Insofar as the perceptual noema is apprehended only by an act of reflection on the "reduced" act, it is not sensuously apprehended. Thus far I agree. However, one may want to specify further the alleged "abstractness" by saying that the noema like the Fregean sense is a linguistic meaning, meaning by "linguistic meaning"

what one *grasps* when one *understands* the meaning of a word or a
sentence. In taking this step one should exercise the utmost caution, for one may reasonably maintain that the Fregean sense itself
is not, in an important sense, linguistic meaning. Furthermore, by
taking the noema unrestrictedly as linguistic meaning, one overlooks the uniqueness of the Husserlian thesis which assigns the
noema to an *act* rather than to a linguistic *sign*. The question,
then, is how can the following three aspects of the Gurwitsch
position be held together without internal disharmony:[93]

(1) that the noema is the *content* of an act (the perceptual noema
is what we are aware of, exactly as we are aware of it, in a
given perceptual act);

(2) that it is an 'ideal', 'objective' meaning-entity, which may be
identical amid variations of acts;

(3) that it *is* the object under a certain aspect and the object is
the system of such noemata.

(1) and (2) seemingly jar, for to be a content of an act is to be
subjective; (3) by reducing the noema to an aspect of the object
obliterates the distinction between noema and object, and by making the object a system of noemata ends up by denying the object
altogether.

However, (1) and (2) jar *only if* one takes 'content' in a nonintentional sense, i.e., in the sense of a *real* part of a mental act. Of
course, what is a real part of a mental act cannot also be an ideal
entity. The noema is not such a real component. It is an intentional content. The peculiarity of the Husserlian thesis is precisely
this, that a real mental act also exhibits an ideal content, i.e., the
noema. As Gurwitsch has emphasized, mental life for Husserl is
not a unidimensional temporal succession of acts (with their real
contents), but a two-tiered structure: a dimension of temporal succession of acts and a dimension of nontemporal meanings intended
in those acts.[94] What, then, to do with (3)? The thesis that the object is *nothing but* a system of noemata is not ascribed by Gurwitsch to Husserl. It is rather his own revision of the Husserlian
thesis, a revision which he undertook with a view to eliminate the
determinable X which Husserl speaks of.[95] I think in this Gurwitsch was wrong. Not only is the X, as the bearer of the noematic
predicates, not reducible to a system of noemata; but what is more,
every noema itself contains, within its structure, the X as the

bearer of the noematic predicates. In any case, the *issue* about the relation between the object and the noemata should be clearly understood. To say that on one interpretation the object is out there, whereas on the other the distinction between the object and the noemata collapses, is to pronounce a rather hasty judgment. One has to begin by pointing out that the noema is not given in the same attitude and the same sort of act, in which the object is presented as being out there. The phenomenological reflection which thematizes a noema also grasps an object *only as* the object of this noema, not as the object *simpliciter* as it was presented in the pre-reflective straightforward act. If *that* object is *now* understood in the language of 'noemata', nothing happens to the original act and its claim to present *its* object. Now in the reflective attitude we speak, within quotes as it were, of "the object simpliciter out there." *This* is a complex sense-structure, a noematic structure. The X itself is a noematic structure. Recognizing the X as an irreducible moment within the noema is not *eo ipso* being a realist with regard to the external object. Nor is it to be an idealist. If for transcendental phenomenology the distinction between 'real being' and 'valid sense' would ultimately collapse, that is not tantamount to denying external objects. It is to recognize that if transcendental phenomenology brackets the object in order to recover its *sense*, that is only a provisional dualism which is progressively eliminated in favor of *sense*. Constitution of sense is also constitution of the object, for, *within transcendental phenomenology*, even "object simpliciter" is a sense-structure. The new discourse does not permit us to recover the abandoned naivete, *save in its own terms*. If I would want to reject Gurwitsch's revision of Husserl's position, that is not because it eliminates the object (for, it does not, it claims to lay bare its constitution), but rather because it removes from within the noema a structural (namely, the X) aspect that should be phenomenologically located there.

What sort of ideal entity, then, is the perceptual noema? On Husserl's thesis, and on both the readings of that thesis, the Gestalt-theoretic and the Fregean, the perceptual noema is not individuated by the temporal occurrence of the act or by the ego whose act instantiates or intends it. Its objectivity is at least the same as intersubjectivity. But then what else could it be other than the sense of the linguistic expression "This wall is blue" in case that sentence happens to express the perceptual act the status of whose sense we are trying to ascertain? On the Føllesdal interpretation, the *emptily* uttered (or, more likely, emptily understood) sentence "This wall is blue" and the *perceptual* judgment "This wall is blue" would have the same *sense,* so that the perception in which the empty linguistic meaning is verified or fulfilled adds nothing to the sense of the sentence. Again, we are led up to the question regarding the justification of Husserl's concepts of "fulfilling sense" and the relation between "fulfilling sense" and "perceptual noema," a question which has just been discussed at some length. The perceptual noema is not itself a conceptual entity, but one that is implicitly conceptual, one that *can be* raised to the level of conceptual meaning, and in fact is a condition of the possibility of the corresponding conceptualization. It is ideal only in the sense that it gives birth to the ideal conceptual meaning.

VII

Three kinds of senses, we have found, resist complete conceptualization, and so linguistic formulation, without undergoing some transformations: the sense of an indexical such as 'I', the perceptual noema, and the sense of an ordinary proper name such as "Aristotle." These three sorts of senses determine our reference to items in the perceptual world qua perceived. These items are individuals and objects of unique reference. Uniqueness of reference is achieved not by a sense alone, that applies to one and only one object, but needs a shared situational context within a familiar world characterized by typicalities.

There is a widely held view that if the sense is to determine reference, as Frege and Husserl thought it did, then the sense must determine reference *uniquely.* In other words, the sense, consisting as it does in a set of predicates, is a description which must be true of one and only one object. The description determines reference, that is, by enabling one, the hearer, to pick out the object of reference and none other. Now I think this is too rigid an interpretation of the thesis 'sense determines reference'. The sense by itself always leaves room for some indeterminacy with regard to the referent. This indeterminacy is removed by perception and by the contextual 'clues'. Even if a description is true exactly for one and only one object, it does not follow that one who grasps the sense, i.e., understands the description, could, merely by virtue of that accomplishment of having understood it, pick out that object. If it were so, reference would have been a part of the sense, and understanding (the sense) would have been equal to knowing (i.e., identifying) the referent.

It should also be noted that the Frege/Husserl concept of sense (disregarding, for the present, the differences between the theories of the two) may be introduced for any one or more of the following reasons:

(1) In order to account for the fact that a sign or an act refers precisely to one object rather than another, in other words as an answer to the question, *how is reference possible*,[96] one needs to suppose that there must be something else associated with the sign, or some component or correlate of the act, which distinguishes the sign or the act under consideration from the other signs or acts which do not have the same reference.

(2) In order to account not merely for how reference is possible, but also for *how the specific mode of reference is possible*, one needs to suppose that signs or acts which refer to the same thing, and yet in different ways, must have something else connected with them which determines the specific mode in which the sign or act refers to its object.

(3) The sense is also needed for filling in the position of the object of indirect, oblique, and intensional discourse, or of reflective acts as distinguished from the naively performed prereflective acts.[97]

(4) The sense is also needed for the role of that which one grasps when one *understands* an expression.

(5) While the preceding four reasons are given by both Frege and Husserl (with appropriate variations to suit their theories), Husserl gives one other reason which one could not expect from Frege. Since Husserl's phenomenological philosophy is especially concerned with mental acts, and the method is one of bringing, through appropriate methodological steps, the eidetic structures of such acts to intuitive givenness, for Husserl the noemata are grasped, in fact intuited, in a special sort of reflection called the phenomenological reflection.[98]

Burge has argued that the sense which is intended to determine reference and the sense which is the determinant of the mode of reference cannot be identical, for the mode of presentation of an object may be insufficient to determine that one object rather than another is the object of reference. Sense, in the first sense, is just not adequate to individuate, independently of the subject's non-conceptual contextual relations to it. Burge's point is well taken; it is indeed closer to the perspective of phenomenology than to that of Fregean semantics. However, the need for several different concepts of sense may be removed by making the first one weaker in the manner I have suggested above. This amounts to saying that although the sense determines the reference, it does not give it unique individuation. With this, one and the same sense may very well fulfill the two roles of (1) determining the reference and (2) containing the mode of presentation of the object of reference. Burge also insists that the sense as determining reference cannot be the same as the sense which is the referent in oblique contexts. His argument is this: when A and B both say "Aristotle was a philosopher," and we report that they said the same thing, we are referring to the sense which is the referent in oblique contexts. But the sense as determined by the context of A's utterance must be different from the sense as determined by the context of B's utterance. Therefore sense as that which determines reference in a certain context cannot be the same as the sense which is the referent in oblique discourse. Again, the argument is flawed, despite the sensitiveness to the cognitive character of the concept of sense and to the role of context in determining reference. The concept of sense as the referent in oblique discourse is that in a sentence such as "A said that p" 'p' refers, not to its truth value (in Frege's theory) or the fact that p (in Husserl's), but to the thought expressed by 'p' in ordinary discourse. If 'p' refers to the thought expressed in its straightforward use, then any name that occurs in 'p' must also be referring to its own ordinary sense. There is nothing troublesome in the view that the sense which 'p' refers to now is the same sense which 'p' expressed in A's original speech which is now being reported. The trouble to which Burge draws attention arises when one reports that A and B said the same thing, for there is no guarantee that the sense they attach to the names occurring in 'p' are identical. But to require that for a sense to serve as the denotation in oblique speech is to require that when both A and B say 'p', they are saying the same thing, is too strong a requirement. The senses they attach may or may not be the same, depending, among other things, on the contextual factors. But even if they mean different things by uttering 'p', whatever each means by it will be the referent of an oblique discourse in which what he says is being reported. If they originally meant the same, then the sentence "A and B said the same thing" would be true, otherwise false, even if they uttered tokens of the same sentence type. So, in principle, I do not see why one and the same entity, the sense/noema, could not fulfill functions (1) through (4).

But it *is possible* that a theory of sense which satisfies the functions (1) through (4) does not satisfy (5), for the sense may very well be a *theoretical* entity that is being posited (to account for the various facts stated in the grounds (1) through (4)) and therefore not amenable to a phenomenological inspection. When Frege says that the sense is grasped, apprehended, or referred to, it would be safe to assume that he is not making out an analogy with seeing an object.[99] But in Husserl's case the analogy with sense-perception is vividly and explicitly on the surface of the texts. Husserl could emphasize such an analogy and the implied intuitionism because by phenomenological reflection—achieved through placing all questions about the reference within brackets—one focuses upon a concrete act of consciousness, a perception, e.g., as whose necessary correlate the *sense* also becomes an object of intuitive apprehension. It is not a *merely posited* entity. It is because of this that I hesitate to try to interpret the Husserlian noema with the help of the notion of "inner representation" so useful in cognitive psychology and functionalist theories.[100]

If the Husserlian noema is open to phenomenological inspection, attempts to understand it as a function from possible worlds to truth values must be fundamentally flawed.[101] Even with regard to Frege's sense, Dummett has rightly pointed out that the notion of meaning as a function which maps each possible world onto the reference in that world is a nonepistemic notion and does not give an account of what it is that someone grasps when one understands a word. I have argued elsewhere at greater detail that the attempt is no more successful as an interpretation of Husserl.[102] Since on such an account the meaning function in question is one given in extension, i.e., simply as a set of ordered pairs [$(W_1, O_1), \ldots (W_i, O_i), \ldots$], all it gives is a *list* of what is "picked out" in each world by noema N. We have no account of why O_i is the image *under* N *of* W_i, i.e., *why* O_i is picked out. We are given nothing in virtue of which O_i is the relevant object in W_i.

To the end of this section remains a question about ontology.

The Fregean theory of sense has led to a sort of ontological embarrassment: the theory commits itself to an infinite hierarchy of senses. Thus there must be not only senses through which we refer to basic individuals such as Aristotle and Venus, there must be senses of these senses, i.e., the higher order senses through which reference is made to the senses of 'Aristotle' and 'The morning star.' Likewise, one must, for the very same reasons, recognize senses of senses of senses, and so on ad infinitum. There is of course no reason as such why such an infinite hierarchy of senses should prove embarrassing. Husserl is also led to a similar hierarchy. Føllesdal quotes an unpublished text which is very Fregean.[103] In the published works there are two clear texts, section 49 of *Formal and Transcendental Logic*, and section 65 of *Experience and Judgment*. To quote only from the latter:

> Sense as sense (the intended content as such) is precisely also an object, or can be made one. . . . As such, it has an objective sense of the second level: the sense of sense is fulfilled in the having of sense. But we then say that the sense lies in the object, that is, the sense of sense lies in the sense, therefore also in a corresponding object; and thus we come to an infinite regress, inasmuch as the sense of sense can by turns become an object, then have a sense, and so on.[104]

The seemingly unpalatable consequence of having to admit an infinite hierarchy of senses is somewhat mitigated, in Husserl's case, by the fact that the senses are correlatives of acts. Since the acts of reflection, or discourse about discourse, can in principle be endlessly reiterated, and since the hypothesis of such an infinite series of acts is not ontologically implausible, the resulting infinite hierarchy of senses may then be appreciated as a consequence of that hypothesis. Apart from the standpoint of acts, the infinite hierarchy of senses is less credible, though not intrinsically muddled or inconsistent.

One way of avoiding such an ontology of senses is to insist that senses qua senses are not objects, they are merely media of reference. But don't they become objects of reference in the reflective attitude or in oblique speech? "Yes," one may reply, "but *as* objects of reference, they are not any longer playing the *role* of senses and so are not senses." (The argument is analogous to Frege's to the effect that 'The concept horse' does not name a concept, that the concept, being predicative in nature, cannot be the referent of a name.) Frege certainly took senses as entities of a sort. Husserl seems to have seen the point as, e.g., when he writes: "Sense and objects—which are not sense—stand in contrast to each other and in essential correlation; they are relative to each other as levels which can always be repeated but which are based on this absolute difference."[105] Senses qua sense are not objects. When they are objects, they are not playing the role of senses any longer.

But, in the long run, Husserl has to admit that there is a sort of reflection, which is called 'noematic reflection', in which the noema is objectified precisely qua sense. The question, then, what sort of entities are the noemata is *almost* unavoidable. Husserl keeps this ontological query *in abeyance* by the self-imposed restraint of a phenomenological philosophy. To be fair to him, I must also add that Husserl will argue that the ontological inquiry with regard to the senses is wrongheaded, for ontological predicates such as "being," "existent," "actual" (and their modifications) are after all constituted in the noematic realm, especially in what Husserl calls the thetic component of the noemata.

It is not, of course, quite clear *what sort of* ontology of senses Frege had in mind. In other words, although they are objects of a sort, and are independent of both the linguistic signs to which they happen to be attached and the mental states of whoever intends or grasps them, in what sense do they possess a being of their own? Dummett wants to understand it in the weaker sense according to which when Frege speaks of senses as eternal, immutable entities, his locutions may be interpreted as emphasizing their *communicability*.[106] The strongest interpretation, also the most widely shared, would be to ascribe to him a Platonic Realism. Sluga prefers, in view of Frege's alleged philosophical affiliations, a sort of Kantian-Lotzean form of idealism.[107] For my present purpose, I need not decide between these. One must bear in mind, however, that Husserl's much-discussed "Platonism" concerns not so much his thesis about the ideality of meanings as his theory of essences. Essences are not meanings.[108] Essences, which Husserl undoubtedly admitted into his ontology (in fact, in strict parlance, for Husserl, all *ontologies* are essentialistic[109]), are entities that have beings of their own. Meanings are, in Husserl's maturer theory, *correlates of* acts.

Husserl's earlier theory, which he proposed in the First Logical Investigation, is ontologically *simpler*. It takes meaning to be a *species* of which the particular acts in which that meaning is intended are instances (the relation, he says, is analogous to that between 'Red' and particular patches of red). The latter theory, according to which meanings are *correlates* of acts, is phenomenologically sounder: it has a better account of what it is one grasps when one understands.

CHAPTER 4

Logic and Theory of Knowledge

In this chapter, I will consider the conceptions of logic and knowledge that we find in Husserl and Frege. Earlier, their rejection of psychologism and theories of sense were evaluated. Rejection of psychologism and a wide area of agreement in their distinction between sense and reference, however, leave room for very different conceptions of logic and also for very different theories of knowledge.

First as to logic. Besides the issue of psychologism, there were two other controversies about the nature of logic in which both Husserl and Frege participated. These were the issue of formalism and the dispute between the extensionalists and the intensionalists. With regard to the former, Husserl and Frege were on the same side, but with regard to the latter, they were on opposite sides. Both were opposed to formalism as a philosophy of logic (and mathematics). But whereas Husserl's sympathies lay on the side of the intensionalists, Frege was an extensionalist. While these characterizations are on the whole correct, they need to be made with caution for reasons that will soon be clear.

(1) Frege launched severe attacks on formalism as a philosophy of mathematics.[1] These criticisms are equally applicable to a formalist philosophy of logic. In arithmetic, formalism amounts to the thesis that "arithmetic is concerned only with the rules governing the manipulation of the arithmetical signs, not, however, with the meaning of the signs."[2] Formalistic theories need no other basis for the rules of the game excepting that the rules are stipu-

lated. Consequently, formalism rids us of all metaphysical difficulties, which is claimed as an advantage of the approach. As against such a theory, Frege defends the notion of "arithmetic with content." In arithmetic with content, sentences such as equations and inequalities express thoughts, whereas in formalistic theories they are comparable to positions of pieces in a game of chess, moved about according to rules of the game and without consideration of any other meaning.[3] Consequently, in such a formalistic theory, there is no question of *truth*, there is only the question of the legality of a move.[4] Frege even goes on to make the point that "in formal arithmetic, . . . time is involved by the subject-matter itself. For while numbers proper are timeless, the numerical figures arise and pass away in time. The manipulations of the game also take place in time."[5] What he shows in his criticism is that the formalist cannot carry out his program consistently, that in the end the numerical figures come to be used *as signs*, that he does not distinguish between the game and the theory of the game, that consequently he surreptitiously borrows concepts from, and even slides back unawares into, arithmetic with content.[6]

In the paper "Über formale Theorien der Arithmetik" (1885), Frege begins by distinguishing between two senses of "formal theory," with one of which he agrees while the other he will refute. According to the sense in which, for Frege also, arithmetic (and thus logic) is a formal theory, all arithmetical (and thus logical) propositions could be derived purely logically from definitions alone. In this sense, to say that arithmetic is formal amounts to saying that it is *logical* in nature. It would be a mistake, however, to ground logic in arithmetic; on the contrary, arithmetic must rest on logic. There is no specifically arithmetical mode of inference which cannot be reduced to the general principles of logic.[7] The logician, therefore, must not borrow his concepts from arithmetic (as Boole and Schröder did), but must deal with the logical concepts and relations themselves. The sense of "formal theory," in which for Frege neither arithmetic nor logic is a formal theory, is one according to which, for example, the numerical signs such as '1/2', '1/3', 'π' are just empty signs, or, rather, these signs themselves are the numbers. Although Frege's *Begriffsschrift* is, in the words of Kneale and Kneale, "the first really comprehensive system of formal logic,"[8] "it strives to make it possible to present a content."[9] "Right from the start," Frege wrote comparing his concept-script with Boole's logical calculus, "I had in mind the *expression of a content.*"[10] The contents (of thought) are to be rendered more exactly than is done by ordinary language. This is why Frege regarded his script as a *lingua characteristica*, and not as a *calculus ratiocinator.* Furthermore, logic may not borrow any of its signs or concepts from mathematics inasmuch as mathematics itself is a development of logic. On the contrary, logic must develop its own signs, "derived from the nature of logic itself."[11] It is more appropriate to say, then, that Frege is the founder not of mathematical logic but of logical mathematics (and of modern formal logic). Obviously, since the contents which the script represents could not be empirical, they are but the purely logical contents. Frege does not make clear what he means by *"Inhalt."* In his later thinking, this would be restricted to the "assertible content," and, still later, within "assertible contents," distinction would be made between sense and reference.[12] Although advocating the idea of artihmetic (and logic) with content, Frege rejects any appeal to 'intuition' in arithmetical proof (and logical inference).[13]

With many of these views Husserl was in complete agreement. In his letter to Frege dated 18 July 1891, Husserl agrees that the *Begriffsschrift* was not a calculus, but a language, and draws Frege's attention to his own similar distinction between the two. In his review of Schröder's *Algebra*, Husserl had written: "Language is not a method of systematic symbolic deduction; calculus is not a method of systematic symbolic expression of psychic phenomena."[14] Consequently he suggests that the *Begriffsschrift*'s subtitle —"a formal language constructed after the arithmetical"—is inaccurate. In the same letter, Husserl comments favorably on Frege's paper "Über formalen Theorien in der Arithmetik." "I am completely in agreement," he writes, "with you in your rejection of 'formal arithmetic' as it is now taken to give us, not merely an extension (and certainly a very significant one) of arithmetical technique, but a *theory* of arithmetic." This remark is puzzling, as indeed are the sentences in the paragraph preceding it. There Husserl writes: "The method which, after much fruitless effort, I have recognized as successful has been discussed by you in your 'Über formale Theorien in der Arithmetik' but not regarded as tenable."[15] The context shows that Husserl is referring to the method of justifying imaginary numbers in arithmetic. In these remarks, Husserl appears to have regarded the formalist *technique* as a successful way of extending the domain of numbers to include the irrational and complex numbers. But in any case, he agrees with Frege in rejecting formalism as a good *theory* of arithmetic. Frege's rejection of the formalist position includes both his technique and his theory.

In a paper from the year 1893,[16] Husserl distinguishes between two ways of doing logic. One of these is the formalistic way. Without having any specific domain in mind, the logician may choose his definitions and fundamental propositions, arbitrarily and purely symbolically. In this case, the concepts and objects to which the calculus will apply are not given to start with. The other way, as opposed to the first, consists in starting from a given conceptual domain, and then in giving the definitions of fundamental propositions entirely in accordance with the requirements of that domain, but never arbitrarily. One of Husserl's complaints against Schröder was that Schröder started out as if following the second way, i.e., with the domain of manifolds (*Mannigfaltigkeiten*), but then proceeded to give purely formal and arbitrary definitions, as though following the first way; and then looked for an interpretation for them. If this is the case, then Schröder mixed up the two ways of doing logic. Frege draws attention to a similar confusion in Schröder's work when he writes: "the pure domain-calculus is quite unfruitful; and its apparent fruitfulness in this book arises just because it is not pure; something logical is always intruding, a thing that happens almost imperceptibly by way of the words 'manifold', 'individual', 'class', 'subsumption'."[17]

A logical calculus such as Schröder's is not itself the logic of that calculus, any more than a universal arithmetic comprehending the entire domain of numbers could also give a logic for itself.[18] An algebra of logic is not by itself the logic of that algebra.[19] Not unlike Frege, Husserl is dissatisfied with the idea that logic should depend upon and make use of arithmetical notions, for it *is prior to* and underlies arithmetic.

In his Foreword to the first edition of the *Logical Investigations*, Husserl says that researches into formal arithmetic and theory of manifolds pushed him toward a universal theory of formal deductive systems. He came to appreciate the possibility of so generalizing formal arithmetic that it is freed from restriction to the domain of quantity, for "quantity did not at all belong to the most universal essence of the mathematical or the 'formal'."[20] He came to

be concerned with, among others, the problem of the relation between arithmetical and logical formality. This was the period during which he was reading not only Frege but also Hilbert. Hilbert
appears to have had great influence on him, and although a purely
formalist philosophy of mathematics had no appeal for him, he
admired the formalist techniques. Eventually, however the concept
of pure logic that he elaborates turns out to be a logic of *contents*,
of pure meanings.

In the First Logical Investigation, Husserl returns to the theme of
formalism.[21] Signs, he argues, are not objects of our thought at all,
"even surrogatively. . . . We rather live entirely in the consciousness of meaning." There is no doubt, as he had maintained in his
Philosophie der Arithmetik, that symbolic thinking, i.e., thinking
in which mere signs do duty for concepts, plays an important role
in arithmetic. But even in "arithmetical symbolic thought," it is
not signs, in the sense of *physical* objects, which are combined,
which are the subject matter for theorizing. He, like Frege, turns to
the comparison of mathematical operations with the rule-governed
games such as chess. "Chessmen are not part of the chess game as
bits of ivory and wood having such and such shapes and colors."
They become "chessmen" by acquiring their fixed *games-meaning*
through the rules of the game. Arithmetical signs, besides their
games-meaning, have their original meaning. In symbolic thinking,
signs taken in their *operational or games-sense* do duty for the
same signs in their full arithmetical sense. As will be noticed, Husserl makes greater concession to the formalist. Frege will have no
such concept of games-meaning or operational sense at all. In sec-
tions 95–96 of the *Grundgesetze*, Volume II, he argues against the
idea that a content is assigned to chess pieces by virtue of their
behavior in accordance with the rules of the game. In section 97, he
adds that if in addition to the proper meaning of numerical signs
one recognized a "formal meaning," there would be danger of ambiguity.

(2) If both Husserl and Frege are on the side of logic (and mathematics) "with content" as against formalism, they are on opposite
sides in the dispute between extensional and intensional logics. As
far as Frege is concerned, any interpretation of his position with
regard to this dispute has to take into account: (a) his views about
the relation between 'class' and 'concept'; (b) his conception of
logic as truth-functional; and (c) his view that logic is concerned,

not with thoughts as such, but with thoughts only insofar as they are true. It is with regard to (a) that his philosophy of logic appears to be nonextensional. In the essay on Schröder, he writes:

> Only because classes are determined by the properties that individuals in them are to have, and because we use phrases like this: 'The class of objects that are b': only so does it become possible to express thoughts in general by stating relations between classes: only so do we get a logic.[22]

The concept accordingly is logically prior to its extension.[23] In a note from 1906 under the heading "What may I regard as the result of my work?" Frege writes: "the extension of a concept or class is not the primary thing for me."[24] In the *Grundlagen* section 51, he rejects the theory that concepts are always acquired by abstraction from things falling under it. One may as well start with definitions under which nothing falls. Even an inconsistent concept has a place in science, for otherwise there would be no indirect proof.[25] Now all this suggests that Frege was an intensionalist in his theory of concept.

Writers on Frege have sought to underplay this thesis about concepts. Thus Dummett thinks that Frege views concepts as extensional,[26] the only difference between concepts and classes being that classes are objects while concepts are not. The difference is one of *levels*. While there is hierarchy of *types* for concepts and functions, no such hierarchy holds good for classes. The reason, according to Dummett, why Frege's concepts are extensional is that Frege defines for them an extensional criterion of identity: two concepts F and G are identical, if they are co-extensive, even if 'F( )' and 'G( )' have different senses. Furth concurs, and adds that the contrary view, that Frege regarded concepts to be intensional entities, stems from a confusion between the sense and reference of concept-words, a confusion which leads one to suppose that after all the concept is the sense while extension is the reference.[27] But the right view, one which Frege never ceased to emphasize, is that concepts are references. Like Dummett, Furth also holds that the only difference between concept and extension is the differences of *saturation:* concepts are not saturated, so not objects, extensions are *objects*. When Frege writes in the *Grundlagen* that "concepts can have the same extension without coinciding," what he means, according to Furth, is that concepts cannot be 'identical' in a sense that is appropriate only for objects.[28] Sluga also holds the same view, with the added sophistication that, according to him, the Fregean 'extension of a concept' is not the class or set as ordinarily understood by laymen and mathematicians alike, but the value-range (*Wertverlauf*) of the concept.[29] The value-range, and not the intuitive class or set, is a logical entity (as contrasted with the mere physical aggregate). Again, the concept is unsaturated, while the value-range is saturated and so an object. Sluga's interpretation, the best of these, is supported by the following text from a 1906 essay on Schoenflies:

> an extension of a concept is at bottom completely different from an aggregate. The aggregate is composed of its parts. Whereas the extension of a concept is not composed of the objects that belong to it. . . . The extension of a concept simply has its being in the concept, not in the objects which belong to it.[30]

We agree that, for Frege, the concept is the referent of the concept-word; further, that besides the class of objects falling under the concept, there is the *extension* of the concept which is but its value-range. The value-range is an object and so complete. The concept is a function, and incomplete. The concept still is not the same as its extension. An (incomplete) function cannot be the same as a (complete) object. Two concepts are said to be the same, if they have the same extension, but this does not make them 'same' in the sense appropriate for objects. We still have not been able to get rid of the intensional nature of the concept. The distinction between 'concept' and 'object'—here as in other contexts—is fundamental to Frege's thinking.

(b) This appearance of intensionality notwithstanding, Frege's logic is truth-functional. If calculation of classes must be founded on calculation with concepts, Frege wrote in 1910, "the calculation with concepts is itself founded on the calculation with truth-values (which is better than saying 'calculation with judgments.'"[31] The context principle accords primacy to the sentence, over the concept-word, to the thought expressed by the sentence over the sense of the concept-word, and to the truth-value (which is the referent of the sentence) over the concept (which is the referent of the concept-word). 'Propositional logic' may be construed *either* as logic of sentences, or as logic of thoughts, or as logic of truth-values. Husserl chooses the second, Frege the third (and Quine the first) alternative. This makes Frege's logic extensional, Husserl's intensional. The extensionalist logicians are right, according to Frege, "when they show by their preference for the extension, as against the intension, of a concept that they regard the reference and not the sense of words as the essential thing for logic." The intensionalist logicians "forget that logic is not concerned with how thoughts, regardless of truth-value, follow from thoughts, that the step from thoughts to truth-value more generally, the step from sense to reference—has to be taken."[32] Once the distinction between sense and reference has been made, Frege's chief concern appears to be reference, rather than sense. *Only insofar as* truth and falsity pertain to thoughts, do thoughts concern logic. This brings us to the next point,

(c) namely, that logic is concerned, not with thoughts as such, but with thoughts insofar as they are true. (It should be noted that the mere fact that logic is concerned with truth-values does not make it extensional. What makes logic extensional is this fact together with the further thesis that the truth-values are the referents,[33] so that 'p' [where p is a sentence] and one of either 'T' or 'F' are synonymous and can be validly substituted for each other in an inference). Logic is "the science of the most general laws of truth."[34] The laws of logic are "an unfolding of the content of the word 'true'."[35]

Husserl's philosophy of logic stands in sharp contrast to all this. We may distinguish two phases in his response to the intensionalist-extensionalist controversy. At first, he contends,[36] as against Schröder, that it is just not true that a logical calculus is possible only on an extensional basis. On the contrary, Husserl wants to show that it is possible to construct a calculus of pure "consequence" on the basis of a logic of intension. Thus, at this point of time, he is not denying that there can be a purely extensional logic. He is only contending that an intensional logic may very well be developed as a calculus, such that it will have exactly the same formulae as a given extensional calculus. The intensional calculus will be one of ideal contents. To Schröder's objection that only a small number of the infinitely many features (*Merkmale*) of a concept can *actually* be given, Husserl replies that the ideal content of a concept is given, or not given, to us exactly in the same sense as the correlative extension: from the extension of a concept, only a small part is ever actually given. But in neither case is actual givenness necessary. When in extensional logic one operates with classes, what suffices is a symbolic presentation. Exactly the same, i.e., a symbolic presentation of the ideal content of a concept, would suffice for intensional logic. Husserl's thesis, then, is: exactly the same algebraic technic, which is the basis of set-theoretic calculi, can be *directly*, without the detour through set theory, used to develop a calculus of intensional logic. Furthermore, the same axioms of which an extensional interpretation is given in terms of relations between classes may be interpreted as stating relations between members of classes or objects of concepts, or also as stating relations between the concepts themselves. Husserl's point is, to repeat, that logic need not be extensional, and that intensional logic is an alternative, at least equally viable, certainly with precisely the same form.[37]

In the second phase, beginning with the *Prolegomena*, Husserl develops the position that pure logic has to be a logic of *senses*. In fact, the theoretical content of any science is said to consist in "an ideal fabric of meanings." Theoretical unity is a unity of meaning.[38] In its fully developed phase, Husserl's theory of logic culminates in a three-tiered structure: at the bottom, the most primary level, pure logical grammar whose task is to lay down the rules determining which sequences of expressions are meaningful and which are not. This would require a determination of the primitive categories of meaning (nominal, adjectival, propositional), primitive forms of composition of meanings (such as conjunction, disjunction, implication), primitive forms of meaning modification (such as the modification of predicative to attributive meaning, or of adjectival to nominal), pure syntactical categories, and laws of operation with meanings. Pure logical grammar does not include the theory of formal deduction. The next higher level of logic is a logic of non-contradiction, which is the propositional logic of the tradition. Husserl calls it the pure apophantic analytic. Theory of syllogism belongs to it. It abstracts from all questions of truth.[39] Analytic propositions are those that allow themselves to be fully *formalized* and be apprehended as specifications or empirical applications of the formal-analytical laws whose validity appears in such process of formalization. In an analytical proposition it must be possible to replace all material terms by an empty formal *something*, without thereby altering the proposition's logical form.[40] In Quine's words, the material words occur vacuously. "In such propositions," as

Husserl also puts it, "what is material is boundlessly variable."[41]
Since no use is made of the concept of truth at this level, the principle of noncontradiction is to be formulated here in some such
manner as: "Of two contradictory propositions p and ~p, one is
excluded by the other." One says that the logical propositions are
tautologous. At this level p is a tautology iff p is consistent with
both q_1 and not-q_1, q_2 and not-q_2, . . . , q_n and ~q_n.

The third level of pure logic is to be a logic of truth. The principles and relationships, defined within the second level, reappear
here with a new interpretation. The principle of noncontradiction,
for example, becomes: "If a proposition is *true*, then its contradictory is *false*." The *modus ponens* which at the second level read:
"'N' follows analytically from two propositions of the forms 'If M,
then N' and 'N,'" now reads: "If 'if M, then N' and 'M' are *true*,
then 'N' is *true*." In general, the subject matter of truth-logic is
"the formal laws of possible *truth* and its modalities." Insofar as
analytic noncontradiction is a necessary condition for possible
truth, pure analytic of consequence-logic must precede pure truth-
logic. Husserl considers this concept of the threefold stratification
of pure logic to be "something fundamentally and essentially new."

At the end, for Husserl, pure logic, by virtue of its essential unity
with pure mathematics, is led to a purely deductive theory of
manifolds.[42] The idea of manifolds is the idea of the object correlate of the concept of a possible theory, determined only by its
form. Since all actual theories are singularizations of corresponding
theory-forms, there should on the one hand be a *form of a deductive theory*—or which is the same thing, of a *deductive system*—
and on the other—in fact, as the correlate of the idea of a deductive system—*a pure definite manifold*, i.e., a province, thought of
with empty-formal universality and determined by a complete
axiom-set. It is in such a conception that Husserl's theory of pure
logic culminates. In effect, pure formal logic is also formal ontology, inasmuch as it is concerned with the pure forms, or rather
formal essences, of the empty region of object in general.

It is indeed difficult to see at what points this elaborately stated
theory of logic comes in contact with Frege's. Hilbert's influence is
markedly present and explicitly recognized,[43] although Hilbert's
formalism is still rejected. In brief, the contrast with Frege's philosophy of logic takes the form: in the one case, i.e., Frege's, the
concept of truth defines the *entire* domain of logic; in the other

case, i.e., Husserl's, it defines a part of logic, the other two parts being defined in terms of the concept of *sense.* Consequently, Husserl's pure logic remains intensional, Frege's logic is extensional.[44] Lest the contrast, as thus stated, be misunderstood, one should add what has all along been evident: namely, that if for Frege truth pertains to thoughts (which are senses), in Husserl's case the logic of meanings *leads to* the logic of truth and so is mediately connected with the concept of truth. In any case, Husserl does not and would not identify pure logic with theory of *inference,* as Frege often does.[45]

We need still to reconcile the following three things Frege says about logic: (i) that logic is concerned with thoughts, (ii) that from mere thoughts nothing follows, and (iii) that logic is theory of inference. The last thesis appears to introduce a psychological element into logic, which the first has so uncompromisingly expelled. Inference, as distinguished from implication, contains a mental element: the premise or the premises have to be known to be true, and asserted, so also the conclusion. The 'therefore', which appears within the structure of inference, indicates this mental process, the transition from the assertion of the premise or the premises to the assertion of the conclusions. Inasmuch as Frege considered logic as theory of *inference,* he had to say (ii) that from mere thoughts nothing follows,[46] that the thoughts not only have to be true, but taken to be true and asserted to be so. Indeed, all the rules of inference in the *Begriffsschrift* are formulated in terms of assertions. A mere sentence, an unasserted sentence, is a name, expressing a thought and naming a truth-value. From a name nothing follows. The premise needs to be an assertion. Although he had seen the close connection between his own conception of 'thought' and the idea of '*Annahme*', Frege does not make use of 'supposition' in formalization of logic.[47] Now, all this leaves the role of false thoughts and indirect proof problematic—an issue which we need not explore for the limited purposes of this essay. What is directly relevant for us is the *seeming* intrusion of a psychological element into logic,[48] and the rejection of a pure logic of senses. Although the idea of reference recedes to the background in the later essays called the *Logische Untersuchungen,* and Frege is more explicitly concerned with thoughts, the conception of logic is not fundamentally altered.

Husserl's conception of 'proposition' or sense of a sentence is closer to the conception of *Annahme*. In the *Formal and Tran-scendental Logic*, Husserl distinguishes between the actual state of affairs and the *supposed* states of affairs *as supposed*, the latter being the proposition: "Judgments, in the sense proper to apophantic logic, are supposed predicatively formed affair-complexes as supposed."[49] Since apophantic logic as a pure logic of consequence deals with senses alone, its domain consists of *supposed* objectivities *qua supposed*.

Why then does Frege introduce the psychological mode of locution into logic? An intriguing answer is given by Sluga. Although the relation between a thought and its truth, on Frege's theory, is independent of human acts of judging and asserting, we cannot *know* if a thought is true without making an act of judgment or assertion. Consequently, "when we explicate laws of truth we can do so only in judgments and assertions. What we can spell out is therefore the subjective relation that we establish between a thought and its truth."[50] In favor of this reading, Sluga quotes the following tantalizing remark from Frege's *Nachlass*:

> Thus the word "true" seems to make possible the impossible, namely, to make that which corresponds to the assertive force appear to be contributing to the thought. And this attempt, though it fails—or, more correctly, because it fails—points to what is peculiar to logic.

In itself, a thought has its own truth-value. *For us*, the only access to truth is in judgment and assertion. There is no objective way of describing the relation between a thought and its truth. Any such description would give the *misleading* impression (as in the sentence "The thought T is true") that the predicate "is true" is a component of the thought expressed by the sentence used to do the description.

However, not all is well with this answer. It does give an explanation of why in a theory of inference (which requires that the premises need to be known to be true) Frege was forced to formulate the rules in terms of *asserted* contents. Frege had to do so, for he could not make 'p is true' a premise. But the real reason for this seemingly psychological locution lies in making of pure logic a theory of *inference*. In a purely deductive system, in order to function as a link in a chain of deduction, p need not be known to be true, and so need not be an asserted content. It would do if it is an *assertible* content.[51]

The purpose of the above remarks is not to suggest that the introduction of psychological discourse of mental acts is as such unwarranted, and that it amounts to psychologism. Once the objectivity of thoughts and their truth-values has been established, the locution of mental acts should not cause any further anxiety on that score. That the locution, in Frege, is dissatisfying is due to the fact that, *in his theory*, there is no way of tying the acts to their contents more intimately than he does, *without yet* disturbing the thesis about the objectivity of the contents. This precisely is the seemingly impossible task which Husserl, throughout his philosophical writings, sought to resolve to his satisfaction. Frege's own thought, in this regard, did undergo a change that is significant for our purpose.[52] In the *Begriffsschrift*, it appears as though the content is obtained by omitting the judgment stroke, i.e., the vertical stroke from the judgment

In that case, thoughts can be said to exist only as contents of acts of thinking, but, to be sure, contents which nevertheless have an objectivity, i.e., an intersubjective communicability. If only Frege had seen this consequence of his position, he would have anticipated Husserl's later position, i.e., the concept of *noema*. But Frege's position changed, in the *Grundgesetze*, to a more uncompromising Platonic realism: the vertical stroke is then construed as attaching to an object denoted by '——A'. The act of judging relates to an independently existing entity.

In chapter 2, I said that Frege had no concept of intentionality. In chapter 3, I pointed out that the Fregean senses remain external to the acts which may be directed toward them. We now find the same situation in connection with the relation between the act of judging and the judged content, i.e., the thought. For Frege, the only alternative to psychologism was a Platonic realism. But while thereby psychologism is immediately *set aside*, it is *not readily overcome*. The mental is condemned to be the merely psychological, and any intrusion of mentalistic discourse holds out a threat of a relapse into psychologism. Only an adequate philosophy of mind, which understands the mental in terms of its intentionality, can truly overcome psychologism, for the mental as such would no longer pose a threat to what was gained by the refutation of psychologism. Frege did not take that step.

II

One of Frege's decisive contributions to logic lies in his theory of judgment. Two of its important components are: (1) the analysis of judgment into act and content; and (2) replacing the subject-predicate analysis of the judged content with the *object-concept* or argument-function analysis. In this section, I propose to consider these two aspects of the theory to bring out how Husserl's theory of judgment stands in relation to Frege's on these and other related matters.

(1) We learn from Carl Stumpf[53] that Brentano, in his lectures of 1866–67, developed a theory of judgment which, in rough outlines, is as follows: In the case of names as also in the case of statements, one has to distinguish between what they *express* and what they *mean (bedeuten)*. The meaning *(Bedeutung)* of a statement is called by Brentano the *Urteilsinhalt* (the judgmental content), which is linguistically expressible in a that-clause. (This is what Stumpf later called "*Sachverhalt.*") In a judgment, it is this content that is recognized or rejected. Accordingly, the form or quality of a judgment is either affirmation or negation.[54] In the judgment of the form 'S is P', we are *not,* according to Brentano, predicating P of S, we are accepting, recognizing, acknowledging the content 'SP', or 'S's being P'.

Brentano also held, in connection with his theory of intentionality, that judgments are founded on presentations in the same way that "emotive acts" are founded on judgments. In order to be able to judge that S is P, i.e., to accept SP, it is necessary that SP be presented. Judging that S is P, then, consists first in presenting SP, and then in accepting it.

This entire theory, geared as it was to support a realistic ontology, was developed in opposition to the reigning idealistic theory of judgment deriving from Kant.[55] According to Kant, judgment is a *synthesis* of presentations having objective validity, a synthesis which is in accord with an objective, normative rule and *not* some contingent law of association. Frege, whose theory of judgment is close to Brentano's, gave an argument why judging could not be a synthesis: if affirmation were a synthesis, he argued, negation would be a separation, which is absurd. In any case, Frege, despite his alleged loyalty to a sort of Neo-Kantianism, rejected the Kantian theory of judgment in favor of a Brentano-like theory according to which:

Thinking = Apprehension of a thought.

Judging = (Inward)[56] recognition of the truth-value of the thought.

Asserting = manifesting or expressing this recognition.

In Frege's theory, *unlike Brentano's*, the distinction between affirmative and negative judgments has no logical merit. Negation belongs to the content of judgment, and not to the act. To judge that S is not P, is to recognize the falsity of SP, which is the same as recognizing the truth of S's-not-being-P.[57] However, as in Brentano's theory, Frege's theory also dissociates the "assertoric force" from the predicate. The assertoric force is indicated by the judgment stroke '⊢————'; the predicate belongs to the structure of the content to which the judgment stroke is prefixed. The "is" of copula, then, is ambiguous. In one sense, it designates the act of judging; in another sense, it is a component of the predicate part of the thought that is judged to be true.

(2) Once judgment is analyzed into act and content, the content, i.e., the thought, may be further analyzed into its component parts. It is here that Frege's logical genius and originality best shows itself. He rejects the easily available subject-predicate analysis as being superficial, subjective, and merely linguistic and grammatical. In its place, he gives us an analysis in terms of object and concept, or (what is the same for him), argument and function. Whereas in the traditional subject-predicate analysis the thought expressed by the sentence 'Socrates is wise' consists of a subject term 'Socrates' and a predicate term 'wise', connected by the copula 'is', in Frege's theory it should be analyzed into a function-sense expressed by the concept-word

"———— is wise"

and an argument, which is the *sense* expressed by the name 'Socrates'. (Note that the components of the thought must themselves be senses, and not references.) The referent of the sentence likewise should be analyzed into the function *denoted* by the concept-word and the object *denoted* by the name.

This is a marvelous theory. Once the assertive force is dissociated from the predicate and judgment is regarded as mere recognition of the truth-value of the thought, the thought can no longer be understood as a synthesis of two elements, subject and predicate. For such a synthesis would require an act which has no place, either within the thought content or outside it. The thought must therefore be a whole such that its parts of themselves enter into a unity without needing a supervening act of synthesis. Frege's theory has the merit that it accounts both for the asymmetry of the name and the predicate expression (which partially salvages whatever is to be salvaged from the traditional subject-predicate analysis) and the *unity* of the thought. Both are accounted for by the thesis that every thought must have an incomplete, unsaturated part and a complete, saturated part, the former being the concept-sense, the latter the sense of the name. The two are made for each other. Just as the name 'Socrates' fills in the empty place in

'———— is wise',

so does the sense of 'Socrates', itself a complete entity, fill in the empty place in the sense of '———— is wise'. Likewise, the referent of 'Socrates' fills in the empty place in the function or concept denoted by the predicate expression. Frege writes:

> This unsaturatedness of one of the components is necessary, since otherwise the parts do not hold together. Of course, two complete wholes can stand in a relation to one another; but then this relation is a third element. . . . [58]

Further,

> the unsaturatedness of the concept brings it about that the object, in effecting the saturation, engages immediately with the concept, without need of any special cement. Object and concept are fundamentally made for each other. . . . [59]

While accounting for the unity of the thought, the understanding of concept as a function, i.e., as an entity with an empty place, and of the object as an argument which fills in that empty place, made it possible for Frege to effectively and perspicuously use quantifiers to indicate generality.

In spite of its originality, and especially its rejection of the Kantian theory of judgment as synthesis, Frege's theory does retain some traces of Kantian heritage. It is not difficult to discern that the concept-object distinction is a remote successor to Kant's distinction between concept and intuition, and that the critical philosopher's dictum, "concepts without intuition are empty," is not entirely without its influence on the modern logician's thesis that concepts are incomplete entities. Also of Kantian heritiage are: the essentially predicative nature of concepts;[60] the consequent priority of judgments over concepts;[61] and the peculiarly irreducible nature of the unity of judgment which cannot be construed as an aggregate of parts.[62]

Let us now turn to Husserl. An early account of his theory of judgment is to be found in the reviews he wrote of the German literature on logic. In the second of these reviews, we find him in agreement with Julius Bergmann (whose *Die Grundprobleme der Logik* he is reviewing) that the concept of judgment is irreducible to any other, that any theory of judgment needs to take into account its uniqueness.[63] Coming to details,[64] Husserl insists that 'is' is *not* a copula which connects 'S' and 'P' in the judgment 'S is P'. Rather, the 'is P', as a nonindependent (*unselbständiger*) but unitary act, is grounded on the act of positing the subject expressed in 'S'. If one can speak of "connection" at all, one should rather say 'S' is connected with 'is P'. However, Husserl wants to keep apart two quite different relations: (1) the relation between the presentation which underlies judgment and the belief which completes the act of judging; and (2) the relation between a simple judgment and a judgment of recognition or rejection directed toward it. Husserl's views, even as early as this, appear to diverge from Brentano's in three respects. First, Brentano and Bergmann held that the presentation which underlies judgment is a nominal presentation of the object denoted by the subject term even if it includes the determinations being predicated. In the case of the judgment 'S is P', the presentation is that of 'S' as possessing, of course, 'P' as a determination. The presentation is nominal, its verbal expression is a name, such as 'The P-possessing S'. It is this which, in Brentano-Bergmann theory, is asserted to be existent. Husserl insists that the presentation underlying a judgment is rather the entire meaning content of the statement, with all its inner structuring and forms, i.e., the entire 'S is P' exactly as it is intended by the statement. The only thing that it lacks, that which, when added, would transform it into a judgment, is *belief*. To every judgment that 'S is P', there then corresponds a mere presentation 'S is P'. This is the "matter" of the judgment to which a quality is then added. The "matter," however, is not as the object would be apprehended in prepredicative experience, it has a predicative structure. Even "categorial forms" such as "some," "all," "if-then" belong to it. In the second place, Husserl also rejects the view that the quality is a recognition or rejection of the presentation. The primary judgment, for Husserl, is a *belief* in the matter. A higher order judgment would be one in which "is true" or "is false" is predicated of the primary judgment. Finally, since the "matter" also contains categorial forms, and is not a merely nominal presentation, Husserl refuses to go along with Brentano in treating all judging as existential.

In the later logical works judging is said to be a doxic positing of a predicative proposition.[65] The predicative proposition is the sense of the presentation which underlies the judgment. The doxic positing is now further explicated: it is not a simple undifferentiated 'belief' attached to the proposition. Even if judging is a single unitary act, it *includes* (a) a positing of the subject, (b) a positing of the predicate, and (c) attribution or denial of the predicate. Thus the categorial act of predication is a *founded* act, founded on partial acts such as the above three. In this sense, judging is a synthetic, many-rayed act; whereas a nominal presentation grasps the whole content in one single ray. Husserl's point here is indeed hard to grasp. On the one hand, there is the predicative proposition 'S is P' which, in judging, becomes the object of a belief (or doxic, positing act). Where then do the component acts come in? They certainly do not form components of the unitary act of belief. Husserl says that the unitary act of judging is a founded act, an act that is founded on partial acts (a) through (c), and that "exists in them as their dominant unity." In order to understand his point, we have to recall that there are two ways in which one may judge. One kind of judging is to assert a proposition that is already "available"; another is to "constitute" the proposition, to perform the act of predication, and then to affirm the proposition so constituted. (Within these two broad types, many variations are possible. For example, one may start by asserting a proposition that is already "available," but then proceed to "do it over again for oneself" by performing the acts through which the proposition is constituted: through this process, one may be progressing from an initially "blind" judgment to a subsequently "distinct," and possibly content-"filled" judgment.) Now the component acts (a)–(c) are the acts on which the categorial act of predication is founded, and the proposition as a categorial objectivity constituted. It then may become an object of a propositional attitude such as believing.[66] One must, then, distinguish between judging$_1$ (in the sense of predicating), and judging$_2$ (in the sense of "believing"[67]). The former alone is an act of active *forming* of the syntactically structured categorial objectivities. The Fregean *sense* is an eternally subsisting entity. The proposition, for Husserl, is a timeless ideal entity, but "constituted" in appropriate acts. Once "constituted," it is "available," forms a part of a "tradition," and can be "reconstituted."

We have noticed Husserl's emphasis on the relation between the founded act and the founding acts. In Frege's scheme, the judgment stroke '├——————' *contains* within it, *as a part*, the content-stroke '—————'. The *grasping* of the thought is a constituent of judging; to the grasping must be *added* the act of recognition of truth-value. Frege's 'grasping' is the same as Husserl's presentation of the proposition. But, is Frege's 'recognition of the truth-value' the same as Husserl's judging$_2$? (Note that Frege has no concept of judging$_2$.) In this connection, three points are relevant.

In the first place, Husserl rejects, after a prolonged discussion,[68] an interpretation of the Brentano thesis (that judging presupposes presentation) according to which a presentation is *contained* within judgment. He writes: "I can find no trace of the required duplicity in act-quality." Further:

> What is questionable . . . is that the *new act really contains the old act whole and entire in itself*, and that, to be more precise, it simply grows out of the old one through the association of the note of belief, the specific quality of judgement, with the mere presentation. . . . [69]

There is no doubt an identical element, but the identical element is not a complete act of presentation, but only an abstract 'moment' of the full act. Judging is *founded on* grasping; it does not contain the latter as a component element.

Secondly, the specific act of *primary* judging$_2$ is, for Husserl, one of believing, not of assent or recognition. *Primary* judging$_2$ is here contrasted with confirmatory judging or judging as confirmation (= judging$_3$).[70] The talk of "assent" is appropriate when we respond to a judgment pronounced by another person. The same is true of "acceptance."[71] Both "assent" and "acceptance" are connected with "fulfillment" and "confirmation," and therefore apply more appropriately to judging$_3$. Judging$_2$ expresses a simple certainty, judging$_3$ a *modalized* certainty, a position-taking, a decision for or against, recognition or refusal. The objective senses "valid" or "invalid" appear as correlates of this modalized, confirmatory position-taking.[72] For science, confirmatory judgments are of central importance.

Third, neither in judging$_2$ nor in judging$_3$ need two irreducible qualities, affirmative and negative, be recognized, for Husserl as much as for Frege. There is only one quality.[73]

How does Husserl account for the unity of thought or proposition? We have seen that, for Frege, the unity is accounted for by the unsaturatedness of one component and the saturatedness of the other. Although Husserl had taken over from the Brentano school, especially from Stumpf, a distinction between 'independent' and 'dependent' meanings (and objects) and worked out for himself an elaborate theory of it in the Third and Fourth Logical Investigations,[74] he did not use Frege's elegant strategy for explaining the unity of proposition. Since he more and more developed the Kantian-looking thesis of the "constitution" of the proposition in subjective acts, and of judging, as a synthetic act of forming, he, like Kant, traced the unity of the *constituted* back to the unity of the judging consciousness. Judging$_1$ is characterized as "a peculiar 'unity of consciousness'."[75] But elsewhere, he also speaks of the proposition as being a whole, which has "forms appertaining to wholeness" and of "a functional unity" of the members functioning within the "self-contained unity of one function."[76]

As noted before, Husserl's theory had all the elements of Frege's more elegant and simpler account. He saw the irreducible nature of the object-concept distinction ("we necessarily come at last to the absolute distinction between concepts on the one hand, and those objects of concepts, that can no more function as concepts, on the other"[77]). He recognized that in 'S is P', the predicate is not 'P' alone but 'is P', which is a "non−self-sufficient part."[78] Why then did he not have Frege's simple solution? Even without appealing to the transcendental theory of constitution, we have an answer at hand: Husserl regarded even the subject term 'S' to be a non−self-sufficient part. The reason he gives for this position is as follows:

If we say, A is b, and continue, A is c, the two propositions do not have an identical member. The same object A is meant twice, but in a different How; and this How itself appertains to the noematic meaning. . . . Occupying the corresponding places in the two propositions, we have differents, each with a content A, that is quite like that of the others; and these contents are formed differently.[79]

Consequently, all members of a propositional unity are non–self-sufficient. The proposition is the *sense*. Its components are *senses*. The sense contains the *How* of givenness of the referent. Even if the same A is being talked about, the A-sense in each case is different. Inasmuch as the A-sense, in each case, depends upon—for the mode of givenness of A depends upon the total proposition—the context, there is no identical A-sense in the two propositions. Although the argument is different, Husserl's position agrees with Ramsey's critique of Frege: the subject term is no less unsaturated than the predicate. With all the members being non–self-sufficient, one looks for the unity either *in* a unitary Gestalt-like form, or in a unity of synthesising consciousness. Husserl looked in both directions.

III

Did Husserl and Frege have their theories of knowledge? At first sight, it appears that in Frege's case we must answer in the negative. His interest was logic and semantics, perhaps a sort of ontology, but in no case epistemology, which he possibly would have brought under the scope of psychology. In the case of Husserl, phenomenology is supposed to have overcome the traditional epistemological problems. Although at least once Husserl formulated his philosophical problem in terms of the *possibility* of knowledge,[80] in subsequent writings this formulation receives less and less importance. However, Husserl regarded his Sixth Logical Investigation as a phenomenology of knowledge. In it, he discusses the nature of knowledge and the concept of truth. In other writings, he discusses the question, how is transcendence possible, and 'transcendental' is explicated as what makes transcendence possible. Although his phenomenology is a new approach to philosophy, it would not be far from the truth to say that a phenomenology of knowledge also deals with some of the classical problems in theory of knowledge, especially the philosophical problem of perception.

As regards Frege, it is true that he is reticent about epistemology, but at the same time it is undeniable that he held and was influenced by certain epistemological convictions[81] and also that he arrived at certain epistemological conclusions of importance.[82] To obtain a vantage point from which we can consider their views about knowledge, it may be best to start from what they obviously had in common—a certain Kantian orientation—and then to follow up the ways in which they departed from and modified that fundamental Kantian position.

The Kantian thesis which both Husserl and Frege acknowledge is embodied in the well-known proposition: Intuitions without concept are blind, concepts without intuition are empty. For both, as for Kant, knowledge is judgment, and judgment is a combination of two heterogeneous elements which in spite of their heterogeneity are exactly made for each other.

That knowledge is judgment Frege states time and again.[83] Merely grasping a thought is thinking, but not yet knowing. Knowing is recognition of the truth of a thought and so is judging. The thought the recognition of whose truth constitutes knowledge consists, as we have seen, of two heterogeneous elements: object and concept. A concept by itself is an unsaturated entity, with an empty place. The object fills this place, and makes possible the complete entity that thought is. If Frege's 'object' plays the role of Kant's 'intuition', then there is yet an important and obvious difference. Although both apparently play the role of 'filling' an empty concept, the Kantian intuition, by itself, is not an object, nor is an object as such an intuition. An object is *intuited*, but to be known it must also be thought. An intuition is as much an incomplete, 'non-independent' entity as a concept is. The Kantian judgment, as an epistemic entity, is composed of intuition and concept. The Fregean 'thought', which is a knowledge-independent structure, has an analogous structure. But the Kantian 'object' is constituted by 'intuitions' and 'concepts' and so by judgments. The constitutive forms of objectivity correspond to the forms of judgment. Does Frege's 'object' stand in any analogous relation to his 'thought', or is the object merely a component of a thought?

In some remarks in "Der Gedanke," Frege appears to go further toward the Kantian position by forging a closer connection between sense perception and thought than his original realism would permit.[84] Starting from the initial distinction between seeing a thing, having an idea, and apprehending a thought, Frege appears to move closer toward establishing a close connection between these three. He asks, how do I succeed in moving from the inner, subjective, private world of ideas or contents of *my* consciousness to the outer, objective, public world of things that we perceive in common? His answer is: "If man could not think and could not take something of which he was not the bearer as the object of his thought he would have an inner world but not an outer world."[85] What he says is that only insofar as there are thoughts (in his sense of the term), i.e., supersensible meaning structures which we can apprehend, is it possible to perceive an external world. The external world is, then, perceived through sense impressions and thoughts.

"Having visual impressions is certainly necessary for seeing things, but not sufficient. What must still be added is non-sensible. And yet this is just what opens up the outer world for us; for without this non-sensible something everyone would remain shut up in his inner world."[86] In this passage, "what opens up the outer world for us" may be construed as "what makes it possible for us to perceive the outer world." This is still realism. The passage quoted just before this one has a stronger idealistic tone, but still allows a realistic construction: there is only this much that one who cannot think cannot move from the inner to the outer world. There would then be no necessary implication that there would be no outer world. I do not think that Frege ever came to the conception of thinking as spontaneous and as constitutive in the manner that Prauss ascribes to him in these texts.

While the original realism is still preserved, it is considerably modified. We *have* ideas, see things, and apprehend thoughts. The first and the last abilities are conditions of the possibility of the second. Only because there are *contents* of consciousness, and one also apprehends objective, timeless thoughts, is one able to transcend those private contents and to perceive a common objective, external world. Apprehension of thoughts, then, is the *a priori* condition of the possibility of empirical knowledge. Prauss is right in emphasizing that to be consistent Frege would have to radically alter his position that thinking is an empirical, merely psychological act, and that any concern with acts would be psychologism.[87] But in developing all the implications of this revised position, one is necessarily led beyond Frege to Husserl.

There is still another respect in which Frege's insights point beyond his achievement. By using the expression 'that lime-tree', Frege writes, "I want to refer to what I see and to what other people can also look at and touch. There are now two possibilities. If my intention is realized when I refer to something with the expression 'that lime-tree' then the thought expressed in the sentence 'that lime-tree is my idea' must obviously be negated. But if my intention is not realized, if I only think I see without really seeing, if on that account the designation 'that lime-tree' is empty, then I have gone astray into the sphere of fiction without knowing it or wanting to." In this interesting passage, two things are worth noticing. In the first place, Frege is speaking of an intention to refer, an intention which may either be realized or not, fulfilled or frustrated. If it is fulfilled, then that lime-tree is not my idea, but an external object. To say that it is an external object is the same as saying that the thought expressed by the sentence 'that lime-tree is my idea' has the truth-value, the False. If the intention is frustrated, the same thought is true.

Second, when my perception turns out to be non-veridical, Frege wants to say that what I thought I perceived is only my idea, and "I have gone astray into the sphere of fiction." This indeed is a remarkable position to take. How can an idea, a content of my consciousness, which, for Frege, is a sense-impression in this case, simulate an external object, be something like a lime-tree? If the lime-tree is not really there, does my perceptual consciousness consist of nothing but sensations and images? Føllesdal has on various occasions argued that since the Brentano thesis of intentionality in terms of act and object fails in the case of non-veridical acts, the Fregean sense should replace the object: in all cases, whether the act is veridical or not, there is a correlative sense, and this is the Husserlian noema. It is indeed curious that when he was faced with the same problem, Frege did *not* use his concept of sense. When my perceptual claim is falsified, what I have before me is of course not a real external object. Frege can replace it only by the *idea*, the real sensory content of consciousness. Why could he not say, it is the *noema*? Possibly because he had no notion of a non-conceptual, i.e., perceptual sense. Husserl, as we have seen earlier, needed this notion. It could play a role which the conceptual sense could not.

In Husserl, the Kantian concept-intuition distinction takes the form of the distinction between meaning-intention and meaning-fulfillment. Knowledge is not a whole in which both concepts and intuitions coexist as parts (as concepts and objects do in Frege's thought). In knowledge, the bare signitive intention is fulfilled, the object that was hitherto merely emptily referred to is now perceived, given, precisely as it was then referred. Mere recognition of truth of a thought is not knowledge. The recognition must be *justified*. Insofar as such justification consists in deducing the thought from other thoughts known to be true, the justification is merely logical. But when in justifying a belief, one appeals to evidence that is not itself a truth, as Frege puts it,[88] one is within the domain of epistemology.

Mere intuitive presentation of an object is not knowledge. Nor is mere thinking so. The thinking must be verified in perception, the signitive meaning intention (whose entertainment is thinking) has to be fulfilled. Without *sense*, Frege writes, we would have no knowledge at all.[89] But apprehension of sense by itself is not knowing. To use Frege's striking metaphor, one undoubtedly acceptable to Husserl, judging (in the strict sense of knowing) is a progression from a thought to its truth-value[90]—shall we also say, from an intention to its fulfillment.

Such a phenomenology of knowledge leaves no room for the talk about faculties and/or sources of knowledge. Using a language that is so nearly Kantian, Frege wants to talk of sources of knowledge. In a late manuscript from 1924/5,[91] Frege distinguishes between three sources of knowledge: sense-perception, the geometrical source of knowledge, and the logical source of knowledge. The logical source has, using Kant's words, no "real use"; on its own, Frege writes, it cannot yield us any objects. Its domain is that of inferences drawn from other known truths. The geometrical source consists in the intuitions, non-sensible to be sure, of space and time (an element of Kantian epistemology in which Frege never lost faith).

In many respects, thus, Frege is a more orthodox Kantian. In others, Husserl's position is closer to the central Kantian thesis which ties together the notions of objectivity, judgment, and synthesis.

CHAPTER 5

Conclusion

We have found that Frege's philosophy is characterized by an ambiguous, rather unstable position in relation to various possibilities. In metaphysics, it is drawn between a Platonic (and common-sensical) realism and a sort of Kantian idealism. In theory of meaning, it occupies an unstable position between a semantic theory (which attaches senses and references to signs) and a semicontextual, cognitivist, epistemological theory (which makes senses and references functions of contexts, intentions, and cognitive perspectives). Its theory of sense also cannot decide between the context principle and the principle of composition: the primacy of the whole sense from which part-senses are abstracted and the primacy of the part-senses out of which the whole sense is to be built up. Its philosophy of mind has glimpses of the full-fledged concept of intentionality, but does not go beyond a logic of intensionality. The mental act is relegated to empirical psychology, and yet the *grasping* of thoughts, as a mental act, is made to account for the possibility of sense-perception. The concept of sense as a necessary correlate of the act is missed just when it could have been discovered, i.e., in case of frustrated intentions. Likewise in the case of logic: thoughts, truth-values, and assertions all claim priority; in the end logic remains an extensional logic of truth-values. Yet the theorems are formulated in terms of assertions. The act of judging remains external to the thought toward which it is directed. Sentences, thoughts, and referents are correlated, *part by part*. No distinction is made between the whole-part relation and the founded-founding relation. In all these respects, Frege's thought leads to Husserl's phenomenological philosophy.

II

Recent Frege interpretation has resulted in correcting one important mistake, namely that the Fregean senses are 'linguistic meanings', if by 'linguistic meaning' is understood either a synonymous expression or the rules for the use of the expression under consideration. The *sense* is rather (1) a cognitive content, but also (2) a timeless self-subsistent entity. It is also (3) the sense *of* a linguistic sign. The task is to tie these aspects together. It appears to me that any attempt to tie them together would require going beyond the limits of what I call below a *mundane* semantic theory which *assigns* senses to signs. One needs to do a phenomenology of sense, which recognizes that senses are, in the first place, senses *of* acts and that the intentional act, despite being a psychological event, has an ideal structure as its correlate or as its content. Such a phenomenology will be able to take into account the contextual and perspectival character of 'intending' an object, without falling back into the privacy of one's inner life.

III

It is indeed fitting that since the Fregean reflection on sense has its starting point in the idea of 'cognitive value', the Fregean semantics *has to be* a phenomenology which reflects on the cognitive content (of an *act*) and cannot be satisfied with comparing the senses conventionally assigned to signs. (In fact, to be able to compare those senses, the senses themselves have to be made contents of appropriate acts of grasping, and one has to reflect on those contents qua contents of those acts of grasping.) To put it another way, it would be odd if a theory concerned with *cognitive* value stopped short with *sentences* and did not focus, through reflection, upon the appropriate *cognitions*. The linguistic philosopher may at this point insist that the only possible course is to determine the sense *of* the sentence expressing the alleged cognition. Since the *sense* contains the mode of presentation, the assumption is that *this mode of presentation* is fully expressed by the sentence. One assumes, in other words, that what one *understands* when one understands the sentence, the *total* cognitive content including the mode of presentation, is *expressed* in the sentence part by part. I want to suggest that a cognitive state always *overflows* the sentence that expresses it, and more is *understood* than is *expressed* in the sentence. This is *not* to suggest that the mode of presentation is ineffable or inexpressible. Indeed, it is expressed in a sentence of the form 'I ϕ that p' (where 'ϕ' stands for a mental act such as 'perceive'), which is other than the original sentence 'p' in which the cognition was expressed. Husserl's thesis of linguistic express*ibility* is retained, and yet one has to look beyond the expression to the cognition. The sentential structure would still provide the clue to eliciting the epistemic structure, but only if it is aided by reflective analysis of one's own cognition. To grasp a cognitive content qua cognitive content, one must, in addition to grasping the sentence's *expressed* sense, reflectively determine the content qua content of that cognitive state. This is how a phenomenological method of reflection should supplement ascertainment of linguistic meanings. The speaker has a prereflective awareness of the content of his own cognitive state; in his *understanding* of the sentence (he utters to express his cognitive state), the sentential meaning is automatically supplemented by the cognitive content he is acquainted with. The auditor has to extrapolate the cognitive content of the speaker from (1) the context and (2) his own idea of what would have been his own content were he the speaker in that context.

IV

Underlying this essay, there is an implied contrast between semantics as a *mundane* science and phenomenology (of language, intentionality, and meaning) as a *transcendental* project.[1] The mundane science begins with assuming the availability of an already 'constituted' world as a world of reference, of senses as media of such reference, and of signs as physical entities. Its task is to connect them within a reasonable theory. A transcendental philosopher will find such a theory interesting, possibly ingenious, requiring some technical virtuosity. But it is not *radical* enough. Indeed, it even presupposes that the entities in the world are objects of reference as much as the timeless senses are just "there" *avail-*

able for use and our "grasping." Transcendental semantics, if I may coin such a phrase, goes back to the *origins* of the phenomena of reference and meaningful discourse (without making use of the all-pervasive world-belief) in the intentional acts of consciousness and their structures. It brings to light *from within* intentionality how meaningful discourse is possible.[2] This is the deeper significance of the contrast between Frege and Husserl.

V

Both the Fregean and the Husserlian theories of objective, essentially communicable, sense are threatened by the indexical expressions, especially by the sense of 'I'. While Fregean semantics is found to contain this inner conflict (the sense of 'I' remains essentially incommunicable), Husserl's theory struggles hard to resolve the conflict by founding communicability on (1) the contextual features of the dialogical situation and (2) the available typicalities of a common life-world. Husserl's theory also has a theory of *perceptual* sense which we have found to be too useful to be deleted in favor of a Fregean interpretation of the 'noema'. The theory of *perceptual sense* (1) provides the linkage between the empty conceptual meaning and the concrete verificatory experience; (2) avoids a naive direct realism, without appropriating perception into 'perceptual *statement*'; and (3) provides the basis on which an account is possible of *de re* intentionality (as contrasted with the Fregean theory which threatens to make all intentionality *de dicto*).[3]

VI

Finally, a few concluding remarks about 'psychologism' with which Frege and Husserl were so profoundly concerned. I have argued that a critique of psychologism that relegates the domain of mental acts exclusively to empirical psychology cannot radically overcome psychologism. Such a position, in spite of its opposition, is constantly threatened by the spectre of psychologism. It is only an adequate philosophy of mind that can radically overcome psychologism. It has also been argued that only a transcendental philosophy of mind, which construes consciousness as being *essentially* transcendental, can achieve this goal.

By way of conclusion, I want to reiterate one point already emphasized in this essay, namely that no philosophy of mind can be strong enough to overcome psychologism unless it recognizes that a large part of the mental consists in intentional acts which have, as their correlates, ideal, time-less structures, the so-called Husserlian noemata or senses. In this context, the following is important: it has been often uncritically assumed that the mental as such is psychological. By 'psychological' may more appropriately be understood a certain *interpretation* of the mental, an interpretation which construes the mental act as a natural event occurring 'within' the mental life of a person, connected causally to that person's bodily states and environmental conditions. An intentional act, construed thus as a natural event, ceases to be 'intentional' *in the strict sense*, it becomes a mental event and inserted into the causal order of nature. At the basis of psychologism, then, is not merely psychologization of the logical entities, of ideal meanings, etc., but, at a deeper level, a 'mundanization' of consciousness. Psychologism, then, is a consequence of this mundanization, and can be overcome only by a recognition of this origin.

VII

What, then, is the 'moral' of this essay? It is that for an adequate theory of meaning and reference, one needs to integrate ideas of Frege with those of Husserl. While Frege's theory worked reasonably well within the limited context of his truth-functional logic, only Husserl faced the "mystery" of the relation of the ideal structures that found logic and knowledge to the mind that "grasps" them. He was able to give an account of this relation which was not psychologistic. For this one needs—Husserl provides us with—a sufficiently rich theory of intentionality and a concept of the mental which is not psychologistic.

Appendix

Frege-Husserl Correspondence*

1. *From Frege to Husserl*

> *Jena*
> *May 24, 1891*

Dear Doctor,

You have, by sending me your *Philosophie der Arithmetik* as also the review of Schröder's *Lectures on the Algebra of Logic*[1] and your articles on the calculus of deduction and logic of contents,[2] given me great pleasure which is all the greater because I myself have been very much preoccupied with these problems. I believe I also notice in your writings, besides some differences from my views, many points of agreement. I have read your review of Schröder's work with great interest, and have been inspired by it now to put down my own thoughts in writing—something I had resolved to do when the second volume would appear. That would perhaps sometimes appear in the *Zeitschrift für Philosophie und philosophische Kritik*.[3] I am in agreement with you when you find Schröder's definitions of o, 1, $a+b$ and $a \cdot b$ defective. Strictly

---

* The letters translated here seem to be the only four that have survived from the correspondence between Frege and Husserl. These four are:

1. Frege to Husserl, 24.5.1891 (original in the Husserl-Archiv, Louvain).
2. Husserl to Frege, 18.7.1891 (original in the Sammlung Darmstadter, Staatsbibliothek der Stiftung Preussischer Kulturbesitz, Berlin, under signature 2 a 1890).
3. Frege to Husserl, 30.10–1.11.1906 (original lost in the war, type copy in the Frege Archive, now at the University of Konstanz, West Germany).
4. Frege to Husserl, 9.12.1906 (original lost in the war, type copy in the Frege Archive).

For appropriate permissions to publish these translations, I am grateful to Professor F. Kambartel, Director of the Frege Archive, and the Librarian of the Handschriftabteilung of the Staatsbibliothek, Berlin.

> J. N. Mohanty, Tr.
> *University of Oklahoma*

speaking, Schröder defines, instead of a+b, $\in$ once again along with
+. One should not, in one and the same definition, define two different things and, least of all, what has already been defined earlier.
The sign $\in$ should have been introduced, at the same time, for all
possible cases. If then a+b is also defined for itself, then it would
immediately follow from it what is to be understood by $'a+b \in c'$.
If with the first appearance of $\sqrt{-1}$ one is left astonished and asking what that means, then that is only an indication of the fact that
the first introduction of the sign for square root was incomplete
and therefore defective. It ought to have been at once such that
there could be no doubt about $\sqrt{-1}$ after the minus sign and '1'
have been correctly explained. Concerning Schröder's argument on
p. 245[4] which you call 'sophistical', I believe to be able to show
that starting from Schröder's foundations one can, in fact, reach his
results as well as yours because two quite different meanings have
been combined in his 'class'. If one adheres to one of these, then
Schröder's o is to be unconditionally rejected. By the way, the algorithm lets itself be retained with suitable determination of the
meaning of ' $\in$ ': but then we shall not be speaking of logic even
remotely. In the other case, the o is admissible, we find ourselves
actually in logical considerations, but intuitiveness is missing, and
the diagrams of Euler are not quite unobjectionable.

But I can only hint at it here.

I would especially thank your for your *Philosophie der
Arithmetik* in which you take similar efforts of mine into consideration in such details as has hardly been done before. Hopefully, I
will soon find time to reply to your objections.[5] Only this much I
would like to say here: there seems to be, between us, a difference
of opinion about how the concept-word (the common name) is related to objects. The following schema may clarify my view:

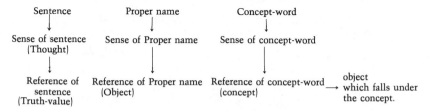

In the case of concept-words, one more step is needed, than in the
case of proper names in order to reach the object, and this last may
be missing—i.e., the concept may be empty, without the concept-word ceasing thereby to be scientifically applicable. I have
drawn the last step from the concept to the object sidewards, in

order to indicate that it takes place on the same level, that objects and concepts have the same objectivity (my *Grundlagen*, § 47).[6] For poetic use, it suffices that everything has a sense, for the scientific it is necessary that references are not lacking. In the *Grundlagen* I had not yet made the distinction between sense and reference. I would now, in § 97, use 'having reference' ('*Bedeutungsvoll*') instead of 'having sense' ('*sinnvoll*'). Also, e.g., in §§ 100, 101, 102, I would now, at several places, replace 'sense' by 'reference'. What I earlier called 'the judged content' ('*beurtheilbar Inhalt*') I have now divided into Thoughts and Truth-values. To judge, in the narrower sense, may be characterized as going over from thoughts to truth-values.

Now it seems to me that the schema, with you, would look somewhat like this:

concept-word
$\downarrow$
sense of the concept-word (concept)
$\downarrow$
object which falls under the concept

so that, for you, the same number of steps are needed to reach the objects from the concept-words as from the proper names. In that case, the only difference between proper names and concept-words would be that the former could be related only to one object and the latter to more than one object. A concept-word whose concept is empty must then be rejected in the sciences exactly like a proper name to whom there is no corresponding object.

I can send you now, in return for your valuable gifts, only smaller writings of mine, to my great regret. From the two lectures on the *Begriffsschrift* you would find that Schröder's judgment (Cp. p. 95 fn., Schröder's *Algebra der Logik*) is unfounded.[7] Certainly, they do not quite correspond to my present standpoints entirely, as you will be able to see from a comparison with "Function and Concept." But since translating into my present terminology is easy, they may still serve the purpose of giving an idea of my *Begriffsschrift*. Instead of 'fact that', one should say 'truth-value of the sentence that. . . ' .

With the hope that the exchange of thought between us will continue and will contribute something to the cause of the science,

I remain
respectfully yours,

G. Frege

2. *Husserl to Frege*

Halle
18.7. 1891

Dear Professor:

Please excuse me that I am expressing my best thanks to you only now for your friendly letter as also for sending me your essays. I did not want to do so without having studied the latter and without further continuing the discussion of the subject matter suggested by you in your letter. Unfortunately, the circumstances were not favorable to my wishes: vainly did I hope to be able to save enough spare time in order to be able to form, what appeared necessary before everything else, a clear picture of the nature and importance of your original *Begriffsschrift*. In this reagrd, I also should not expect too much in the coming weeks, and so I will not any further postpone my reply.

First of all, I may be permitted to mention the great stimulation and challenge that I have derived from your *Grundlagen*. Amongst the many works that were before me during the preparation of my book, I could not name any one which I studied with nearly as much pleasure as yours. Even if I could not agree with your theories in the main points, I was constantly delighted with the ingenious originality, clarity and, if I may say so, the fairness of your investigation which is never too particular, does not pass over any objection, which is averse to all confusion in thought and word, and above all tries to press forward to the ultimate fundamentals.

It is therefore obvious that I have long since entertained the desire to get acquainted with your other works, and I thank you very much that by sending me a whole series of them, especially one which I had tried in vain to secure ("Über formale Theorien in der Artihmetik"), you have made them accessible for my studies.

I also noticed that in spite of essential points of divergence, our insights touch each other in several ways. Many observations which forced themselves upon me, I now find to have been expressed by you many years earlier. How excellently you say, e.g., ("Über den Zweck der Begriffsschrift"): "The problems with which Boole is concerned indeed appear, to a great extent, to have been devised for the purpose of being resolved with the help of his formulae."—Compare my review p. 278.[8] Also the essential distinction, on which I lay stress on p. 258, between *language* and *calculus*, has already been made by you on p. 2 when you separate "*calculus ratiocinator*" and "*lingua characteristica*" from each other.[9] To be sure, it appears to me that the *Begriffsschrift*, since it is meant to be a "*lingua characteristica*," should not be called "a formal language constructed after the arithmetical." For it should be certain that arithmetic is a "*calculus ratiocinator*" and not a "*lingua characteristica*."

I have not yet read Schröder's criticism of your *Begriffsschrift*. That he has not, as you write, done justice to you, I understand very well. He lacks what is indispensable for investigation in the field under consideration: logical subtlety and sharpness. His strength lies in quite another direction. He is a brilliant arithmetical technician, but also nothing more.

I have not yet, to my regret, been able to make use of your pertinent communications, for at present I lack a thorough knowledge of your appropriate works. Thus, for example, I do not have a correct idea of how you would justify the imaginary number in arithmetic. The method which, after much fruitless effort, I have recognized as successful has been discussed by you in your "Über formale Theorien in der Arithmetik" but not regarded as tenable. During this summer vacation I hope to be able to work out my projects with regard to this matter. I may perhaps then succeed in putting together the essentials of my theory in a brief letter.

I am completely in agreement with you in your rejection of "formal arithmetic" as it is now taken to give us, not merely an extension (and certainly a very significant one) of arithmetical technique, but a *theory* of arithmetic.[10] Particularly misleading in this respect has been the well known, but from the logical point of view totally confused, book by Hankel. The English, as I learn, seem to be much clearer—especially Peacock. Unfortunately, I have not yet been able to procure Peacock's famous *Algebra* (1845). Likewise also Gregory's works. Some criticisms of their theories I recently found in the truly praiseworthy booklet by Fine (*The Number System of Algebra.* Boston & New York, 1891).

With expressions of the highest regard,
Yours,

Dr. E. G. Husserl

3. *Frege to Husserl*

Jena
30.10—1.11. 1906

Dear Colleague!

While I thank you very much for your friendly gifts, permit me to communicate to you some observations which have occurred to me while going through them since I do not now have the time to comment on them in a thoroughgoing manner.

The logicians make many distinctions amongst judgments which appear to me to be irrelevant for logic; on the other hand, they do not make many distinctions which I hold to be important. The logicians, it seems to me, adhere too much to language and grammar, and are too much caught up in psychology. That prevents them from studying my *Begriffsschrift* which yet could have had a liberating effect. Rightly does one find that the psychic processes are not truly represented through the *Begriffsschrift*; for that is not also its purpose. If it gives rise to entirely new psychic processes, that also is not what it aims at. One even now always takes it to be the task of logic to study certain psychic processes. Logic has in reality as little to do with this as with the movement of heavenly bodies. Logic, in no way, is a part of psychology. The pythagorean theorem expresses the same thought for all men, while each person has his own representations, feelings, resolutions which are different from those of every other person. Thoughts are not psychic structures, and thinking is not an inner producing and forming, but an apprehension of thoughts which are already objectively given. One ought to make only such distinctions as are relevant for logical laws. No one would, in the mechanics of gravitation, distinguish bodies according to their optical properties. One does not distinguish, or distinguishes too little, between object and concept. Naturally, if both are representations in the psychological sense, there is hardly a distinction to take note of.

Connected with it is the distinction between concepts of first and second order which is very important, but who among the logicians knows anything of it? One must in logic resolve to consider equipollent sentences as different only in form. After the assertive force with which they are expressed has been abstracted from, equipollent sentences have something in common in their contents, and this is what I call the thought expressed by them. This alone is relevant for logic. The rest is what I call coloring

(*Färbung*) and illumination (*Beleuchtung*) of the thought. When one resolves to take this step, one sets aside, with one stroke, a mass of unnecessary distinctions and an occasion for countless controversies for which there is, in most cases, no objective solution. And one gets a free road for genuine logical analyses. Psychologically considered, the sentence that is analyzed is naturally always different from that into which it is analyzed, and one can prevent every logical analysis with the objection that two sentences are only equipollent as long as this objection is recognized. For, a clearly recognizable line of distinction between merely equipollent and congruent sentences cannot be drawn. Even sentences which, when lying in print, appear congruent can be expressed with differing emphasis and are not then in every respect equivalent (*gleichwertig*). Only after an authentic logical analysis has first been made possible, the logical elements may be discerned and the thicket will begin to clear up. For every system of equipollent sentences one needs to have only one unique normal sentence, and one can communicate every thought with these normal sentences. With one normal sentence, one would have every one of the entire system of equipollent sentences, and could pass over to any arbitrarily chosen one amongst them whose illumination (*Beleuchtung*) promised something special for it.

It cannot be the task of logic to follow language and to ascertain what lies in the linguistic expression. Any one who wants to learn logic from language is like an adult who wants to learn how to think from a child. As men formed the language, they found themselves in a state of childlike, picture thinking. Languages are not made in accordance with logical rulers. Besides, the logical in language appears to be concealed under images which are not always correct. In an earlier stage of language formation, so it seems, there took place an excessive degree of exuberant growth of linguistic forms. A later time again had to lay aside and simplify many of them. The main task of the logician consists in liberation from language and in simplification. Logic shall be the judge over the languages. One should do away, in logic, with the subject and the predicate; or one should restrict these words to the relation of an object's falling under a concept (subsumption). The relation of subordination of one concept under another is so different from that (relation of subsumption), that it is not permissible to speak here also of subject and predicate.

Regarding the sentences connected by 'and' and 'neither-nor', I agree with you in essential points. I would put it thus: to the connection of two sentences through 'and' there corresponds the combination of two thoughts to one—to which as a whole a negation can be extended, which as a whole may also be recognized as true.

With regard to the question, whether the sentence 'If A then B' is equipollent with the sentence 'It is not A without B', the following has to be said. In the hypothetical sentence connection, we have as a rule improper sentences of the type that neither the antecedent sentence (*Bedingungssatz*) by itself nor the consequent sentence (*Folgesatz*) by itself expresses a thought but only the entire sentential structure (*Satzgefüge*). We have then in each of the sentences a constituent which only indicates, and these point to each other (*tot-quot*). In mathematics, such constituents are often letters ("If $a > 1$, then $a^2 > 1$"). The entire sentence acquires thereby the character of a law, namely universality of content. But first let us once accept that the A and B represent proper (*eigentliche*) sentences. Then there are no cases where A is true and others in which A is false; but either A is true or A is false; *tertium non datur*. The same holds good of B. We have then four combinations:

> A is true and B is true
> A is true and B is false
> A is false and B is true
> A is false and B is false

Of these, the first, third and fourth are compatible with the sentence "If A then B"; the second is not. The negation yields then: A is true and B is false, or: A is true without B being true—exactly the same as the right-hand side.

If we secondly assume that the letters A and B stand for improper sentences, then for A and B we may better write "$\phi(a)$ and "$\psi(a)$", where a is the component that only indicates. The sentence "If $\phi(a)$, then $\psi(a)$" has now a generality of content, and negation abolishes this generality and says that there is an object (let us say, Δ) such that $\phi(\Delta)$ is true and $\psi(\Delta)$ is false. That is precisely what you mean by the words "A can be true without B being true." The sentence "$\phi(a)$ is not true, without $\psi(a)$ being true" is now to be understood as: "In general, whatever a may be, $\phi(a)$ is not true unless $\psi(a)$ is." Its negation yields: "Not universally, whatever a may be, $\phi(a)$ is not true without $\psi(a)$." In other words, "There is at least one object (say, Δ) such that $\phi(\Delta)$ is true, while $\psi(\Delta)$ is false." We get the same as on the left-hand side. In any case, we have equipollence. If one consults my already 28-year-old *Begriffsschrift* one immediately finds the answer to such a question. Are the sentences now also congruent? One may dispute over this, well, for a century longer. At least I do not see which criterion shall give us an objective answer.

I find however that a question for whose solution there is no objective criterion has no place at all in science.

With respectful greetings,
Your sincerely,

G. Frege

4. *Frege to Husserl*

Jena 9.12.1906

Dear Colleague!

I thank you very much for your letter of 16.11, which leads me to make the following remarks.

It seems to me necessary to have an objective criterion for recognizing a thought as being the same, because in the absence of such a criterion logical analysis is not possible. In order now to decide whether the sentence A expresses the same thought as the sentence B, the following seems to me to be the only possible means, whereby I assume that neither of the two sentences contains a logically evident sense-component. If, namely, both the assumption that the content of A is false and that of B is true and the assumption that the content of A is true and that of B is false, lead to a logical contradiction without it being necessary to determine whether the content of A or that of B is true or false and without using other than purely logical laws, then nothing can belong to the content of A, so far as it is capable of being true or false, which did not also belong to the content of B; for any such surplus in the content of B would lack justification, and according to the assumption, any such surplus would not also be logically evident. Likewise, according to our assumption, nothing can belong to the content of B, insofar as it is capable of being judged true or false, which did not also belong to the content of A. What, then, in the contents of A or B can be judged as true or false fully coincide, and this alone is relevant for logic, and this is what I call the thought expressed by A as also by B. One may, of course, count various things as belonging to the content of A, e.g., a mood, feelings, representations; but all this is not judged as true or false. Fundamentally, it concerns logic as little as whatever is not capable of being judged morally good or bad concerns ethics. Is there any other means of deciding what in the content of a sentence is subject to logic, when two sentences express the same thought? I believe not. If there is no such means, one can endlessly dispute, without results, over logical questions.

Further, I have doubts about the following. You write: "The form with 'All' is normally so understood that the existence of objects that come under the terminal concepts is co-intended (*mitgemeint*) and is presupposed as agreed upon." To me, it appears that the sense that you would like to express is reached only when the word 'co-intended' (*mitgemeint*) is struck off. If existence were meant along with it, then the negation of the sentence 'All *m* are *n*' would be 'There is an *m* which is not *n*; or there is no *m*'. This, however, as it appears, is not what you want. Existence is certainly presupposed as agreed upon, but not co-believed.[11] Now I use the form with 'All' in such a manner that I neither co-intend existence nor presuppose it as agreed upon. The linguistic usage cannot here unconditionally decide, because we are not concerned with what the linguistic usage is. In logic, we may rather fix linguistic usage in accordance with logical needs. The basis for my decision is simplicity. It is inexpedient to use a form of expression like the one with 'All' which one will employ as a basic form in logical considerations in such a manner that thereby two distinct thoughts are simultaneously expressed in a sentence which does not consist in two sentences connected by 'and'. One should always strive after going back to the elements, the simple. It must be possible to express the main thought also without the secondary thoughts. I will not therefore co-intend the secondary thought of existence when I use the form containing 'All'.

Sincerely yours,

G. Frege

Translator's Notes

1. E. Husserl, "Review of E. Schröder's *Vorlesungen über die Algebra der Logik*" in *Göttingische gelehrte Anzeigen*, 1891, no. 7, pp. 243–78.

2. E. Husserl, "Der Folgerungscalcul und die Inhaltslogik," in *Vierteljahrsschrift für wissenschaftliche Philosophie*, Vol. 15, 1891, pp. 168–89, 351–56.

3. However, this review by Frege appeared under the title "Kritische Beleuchtung einiger Punkte in E. Schröders *Vorlesungen über die Algebra der Logik*" in *Archiv für systematische Philosophie*, I, 1895, pp. 433–56. (E. Tr. by Peter Geach in Geach and Black, *Translations from the Philosophical Writings of Gottlob Frege*, Oxford: Blackwell, 1952).

4. Schröder, at this point in his *Algebra der Logik*, criticizes Boole's 'universal interpretation' of '1' and seeks to deduce an absurdity from it (pp. 245–46). Schröder's argument is as follows: if we understand by *a* the class of all those classes which are equal to 1 (when 1 includes all possible conceivable objects), then *a* includes in fact only one object, namely 1 itself and so also the totality of entities which constitute the denotation of 1. Besides, there is also another thing which belongs to *a*, namely 0, for 0 belongs to all classes. Now, since 1 and 0 constitute the class of all those objects which are equal to 1, then we must have not only 1 = 1, but also 0 = 1. For a predicate which is true of a class (in this case, the predicate of being equal to 1) must be true of every individual of this class. In a domain where 0 = 1, every possible distinction between two classes or between two individuals would be, *ab initio*, void (Schröder, p. 245).

Let us see Husserl's criticism of this argument which he calls 'sophistical'. Husserl writes: "If we build the class *K* whose *elements* themselves are classes and indeed those classes which are = 1, then of course *K* contains the class 1 as an element, since 1 = 1. But does *K* also contain the class 0 as *element*? Not at all. By all means it, like any other class, does contain 0 — but only as a subordinate class and not as an element. Of all *elements* of the class *K* it holds good, according to definition, that they are = 1, but the same does not hold good of its subordinate *classes*. Therefore 0 is not = 1. The elements of the null class are, to be sure, also elements of *K*, and of them again it holds good that they are = 1. But this also agrees with their sense as objects of the class of non-existents." (*Gött. gel. Anz.*, p. 272)

From this discussion as well as from Schröder's own suggestions, Husserl draws the following lessons: ". . . in cases where, beside a certain class, also classes of this class appear simultaneously, the calculus should not be blindly applied. In the sense of calculus of sets, every set ceases to be a set as soon as it is considered as an element of another set; and this again is to be admitted as a set only in relation to its primary and proper elements, not, however, in relation to the possible elements of these elements." (p. 272)

Thus Husserl is insisting on a lack of distinction, in Schröder, between the relation of class-inclusion and the relation of class-membership. Frege,

127

in his review of Schröder, as also at other places much earlier, emphasizes this distinction. Husserl considers Schröder's *'o'* to be 'schöpeferische.' (p. 269) Frege writes later: "Schröder ventures to invent an empty class." (*Grundgesetze der Arithmetik, Begriffsschriftlich abgeleitet,* 1893; E. Tr. by M. Furth, *The Basic Laws of Arithmetic,* University of California Press, 1964, esp. p. 31.)

5. Frege's review of Husserl's *Philosophie der Arithmetik* was published in *Zeitschrift für Philosophie und philosophische Kritik,* 103, 1894, pp. 313–32. (E. Tr. by E. W. Kluge in: *Mind,* July, 1972, pp. 321–37).

6. This statement by Frege clearly shows that the view that Frege did not have a theory of 'reference' with regard to concept words—that there *'Bedeutung'* is the same as what is *'Sinn'* in the case of proper names, is mistaken. Dummett and Furth have rightly criticized this Frege-interpretation.

7. Schröder writes on p. 95 of his book: "Das Herrn Freges "*Be-griffsschrift*" diesen ihren Namen nicht verdient, sondern etwa als eine in der That Logische (wenn auch nicht zwechmässigste) Urteilsschrift zu be-zeichnen wäre, glaube ich in meiner Rezension dargethan zu haben." (footnote)

In his 1882 "On the Scientific Justification of a Conceptual Notation" (E. Tr. under this title by Terrell Ward Bynum in: Frege, *Conceptual Notation,* Oxford, 1972), to which Frege is referring here, he has already replied to the same objection earlier made by Schröder (in the latter's review of the *Begriffsschrift*). There Frege writes: "Schröder says that my (conceptual notation) has almost nothing in common with Boole's calculus of concepts, but it does with his calculus of judgments. In fact, it is one of the most important differences between my mode of interpretation (*Auffas-sungsweise*) and the Boolean mode—and indeed I can add the Aristotelian mode—that I do not proceed from concepts, but from judgments. But this is certainly not to say that I would not be able to express the relation of subordination between concepts." (p. 94)

8. Schröder had complained in his 1880 review of Frege's *Begriffsschrift* that Frege had failed to take into account the achievements of Boole, whose formal language is, in Schröder's view, preferable to Frege's. In response to this criticism, Frege writes in his "On the aim of the 'conceptual Notation'": "This reproach, however, essentially overlooks the fact that my aim was different from Boole's. I did not wish to present an abstract logic in formulas, but to express a content through written symbols in a more precise and perspicuous way than is possible with words. In fact, I wished to produce, not a mere *calculus ratiocinator,* but a *lingua char-acteristica* in the Leibnizian sense. In doing so, however, I recognize that deductive calculus is a necessary part of a conceptual notation. If this was misunderstood, perhaps it is because I let the abstract logical aspect stand too much in the foreground." (*Conceptual Notation.* E. Tr. and ed. by Ter-rell Ward Bynum, p. 90–91) (Günther Patzig points out that the expression 'lingua characteristica' is not Leibniz's, but comes from R. E. Raspe's edi-tion of "Oeuvres philosophiques de Leibniz" where the editor introduced it as a title. Leibniz's expression was 'lingua rationalis'. *Cf.* Günther Pat-zig's *Einleitung* to his edition of Frege's *Logische Untersuchungen,* Göt-tingen: Vandenhoeck & Ruprecht, 1966, esp. p. 10 fn. 8)

Husserl agrees with this self-interpretation of Frege. Also see Husserl, "Antwort auf die vorstehende "Erwiderung" des Herrn Voigt" in: *Viertel-*

jahrsschrift für wissenschaftliche Philosophie, Vol. 17, pp. 508–511, esp. 511.

9. The distinction to which Husserl is here referring is contained in the following sentences from his review of Schröder: "... the fundamental error rests on a lack of appreciation of the essential distinction between language and algorithm ... Language is not a method of systematic symbolic deduction; calculus is not a method of systematic symbolic expression of psychic phenomena." (*Gött. gel. Anz.*, 1891, p. 258)

10. This was published in the *Sitzungsberichte der Jenaischen Gesellschaft für Medizin und Naturwissenschaft* für das Jahr 1885, Jena: Fischer, 1885/86, pp. 94–104 (Reprinted in Ignacio Angelelli (ed.), *Freges Kleine Schriften*, Hildesheim: Georg Olms, 1967, pp. 103–11). The sense of 'formalism' in which Frege rejects it as a theory of arithmetic is that according to which the signs for numbers like '½', '¼', 'π' are empty, meaningless signs (*leere Zeichen*). According to this theory, as Frege seems to understand it, these empty signs themselves are the numbers; they constitute the proper subject matter of arithmetic.

11. Husserl holds the view that the universal judgment "All *ms* are *n*" *presupposes* the exitence of objects referred to by '*m*'. Compare P. F. Strawson: "... the existence of members of the subject-class is to be regarded as presupposed (in the special sense described) by statements made by the use of these sentences" (*Introduction to Logical Theory*, London: Methuen, 1952), p. 176. There are obvious differences between the two views.

Notes

1. Historical Considerations

1. E. Husserl, *Philosophie der Arithmetik*, I. *Psychologische und Logische Untersuchungen* (Halle: Pfeffer, 1891); *Husserliana*, Vol. XII, ed. L. Eley (The Hague: Martinus Nijhoff, 1970).

2. G. Frege, "Rezension von E. Husserl, *Philosophie der Arithmetik*," *Zeitschrift für Philosophie und philosophische Kritik*, 103 (1894): 313–332; "Review of Dr. E. Husserl's Philosophy of Arithmetic," trans. E.W. Kluge, in: *Mind*, LXXXI (1972):321–337; repr. in J.N. Mohanty, ed., *Readings on Edmund Husserl's "Logical Investigations"* (The Hague: Martinus Nijhoff, 1977), pp. 6–21.

3. E. Husserl, *Logische Untersuchungen*, I. *Prologomena zur reinen Logik* (Halle: Max Niemeyer, 1900). *Logical Investigations*, trans. J.N. Findlay, Vol. I (New York: Humanities Press, 1970).

4. Husserl, *Logical Investigations*, I. p. 47.

5. D. Føllesdal, *Husserl und Frege* (Oslo: Aschehoug, 1958), p. 23.

6. Ibid., p. 25.

7. R.C. Solomon, "Sense and Essence: Frege and Husserl," *International Philosophical Quarterly*, 10 (1970):380.

8. E. Husserl, "Besprechung: E. Schröder, *Vorlesungen über die Algebra der Logik*, I," *Göttingische gelehrte Anzeigen* (1891):243–278.

9. E. Husserl, "Der Folgerungskalkül und die Inhaltslogik," *Vierteljahrsschrift für wissenschaftliche Philosophie*, 15 (1891):168–189, 351–356.

10. Husserl, *Logical Investigations*, I, p. 322.

11. Thus Frege writes: "First of all, everything becomes presentation. The references of words are presentations. . . . Objects are presentations . . . concepts, too, are presentations." A little later on: "Everything is shunted off into the subjunctive" ("Review of Husserl's *Philosophy of Arithmetic*").

12. H. Dreyfus, "The Perceptual Noema: Gurwitsch's Crucial Contribution," in *Life-World and Consciousness: Essays for Aron Gurwitsch*, ed. L. Embree (Evanston, Ill.: Northwestern University Press, 1972), pp. 139–140. In a footnote on p. 140, Dreyfus rejects Gurwitsch's claim that Husserl discovered the distinction between real mental states and ideal meanings and refers to "Husserl's explicit attribution of this distinction to Frege" (*Logical Investigations*, I, p. 292). This reference, however, is misleading. First, this is not the place where Husserl first introduces the distinction. The distinction was first introduced in the 1891 Schröder review, as this paper will argue. Second, Husserl is only referring to Frege's different terminology.

13. Husserl, "Besprechung: E. Schröder, *Vorlesungen* . . . ," p. 250.

14. Thiel considers the terminology of 'sense' and 'reference' obligatory for all Frege works after 1890. Cf. C. Thiel, *Sense and Reference in Frege's Logic* (Dordrecht: Reidel, 1968), p. 44. Angelelli finds the distinction already present in *the Begriffsschrift* ("only the famous terminology . . . is

lacking here"} and in the *Grundlagen*, §67. Cf. I. Angelelli, *Studies on Gottlob Frege and Traditional Philosophy* (Dordrecht: Reidel, 1967). G. Frege, *Begriffsschrift, eine der arithmetischen nachgebildete Formelsprache des reinen Denkens* (Halle, 1879), trans. T.W. Bynum in: *Frege's Conceptual Notation* (Oxford: Clarendon Press, 1972), and idem, *Die Grundlagen der Arithmetik. Eine Logisch-mathematische Untersuchung über den Begriff der Zahl* (Breslau, 1884), trans, J.L. Austin: *Foundations of Arithmetic*, 2nd rev. ed. (Evanston: Northwestern University Press, 1968).

15. Husserl, "Besprechung: E. Schröder, *Vorlesungen* . . . ," pp. 258–259.

16. Ibid., p. 247.

17. Ibid., p. 246.

18. Husserl, "Folgerungskalkül und Inhaltslogik," pp. 169, 171.

19. Husserl, "Besprechung: E. Schröder, *Vorlesungen* . . . ," p. 257.

20. Ibid., p. 262.

21. Husserl, "Folgerungskalkül and Inhaltslogik," p. 178.

22. Husserl, "Besprechung: E. Schröder, *Vorlesungen* . . . ," p. 249.

23. Husserl, *Logical Investigations*, I, pp. 322–325.

24. Ibid., p. 69.

25. Ibid.

26. Ibid., p. 244.

27. Ibid.

28. Ibid., p. 245.

29. Ibid.

30. G. Frege, "Kritische Beleuchtung einiger Punkte in E. Schröders Vorlesungen über die Algebra der Logik," *Archiv für systematische Philosophie*, I (1895):433–436.

31. G. Frege, "Über den Zweck der Begriffschrift," *Jenaische Zeitschrift für Naturwissenschaft*, XVI (1883), Supplement, pp. 1–10.

32. G. Frege, "Über formale Theorien der Arithmetik," *Sitzungsberichte der Jenaischen Gesellschaft für Medizin und Naturwissenschaft für das Jahr 1885* (Jena: Fischer, 1885–86), pp. 94–104, repr. in *Freges kleine Schriften*, I. Angelelli, ed., (Hildesheim: Georg Olms, 1967), pp. 103–111.

33. *Freges kleine Schriften*, p. 105.

34. I am indebted to Professor F. Kambartel of the University of Konstanz, Director of the Frege-Archiv, for making these available to me.

35. See n. 30 above.

36. *Freges kleine Schriften*, p. 207.

37. Ibid., p. 208.

38. Ibid., p. 209.

39. Ibid., pp. 209–210.

40. "Ausführungen über Sinn und Bedeutung," in G. Frege, *Nachgelassene Schriften*, ed. H. Hermes, F. Kambartel, and F. Kaulbach (Hamburg: Felix Meiner, 1969), pp. 128–136.

41. Ibid., p. 134.

42. Ibid., p. 133.

43. Ibid.

44. E. Husserl, "Persönliche Aufzeichnungen," ed. W. Biemel, in *Philosophy and Phenomenological Research*, XVI (1956):293–302, esp. p. 204. Emphasis mine.

45. To my 1974 article "Husserl and Frege: A New Look at Their Relationship" (which is incorporated, with some changes, in this portion of

this chapter), Dagfinn Føllesdal has written a response, "Husserl's Conversion from Psychologism and the *Vorstellung*-Meaning Distinction—Two Separate Issues," which will appear, together with my earlier paper, in H. Dreyfus, ed., *Husserl, Intentionality and Cognitive Science* (Cambridge, Mass.: M.I.T. Press, forthcoming). Føllesdal's main contention is that while it is true that Husserl arrived at the *Vorstellung* meaning-reference distinction independently of Frege's influence, this distinction by itself does not amount to rejection of psychologism. For the latter, Føllesdal insists, Frege's 1894 review was a decisive influence. However, the psychologism Frege attacks in his 1894 review is precisely one that reduces everything, meanings and objects, to *Vorstellungen*. If Husserl had already seen that neither meanings nor objects are *Vorstellungen*, Frege's attacks, even if justified as against the *Philosophy der Arithmetik*, could not have had the influence one might think they had. Although Husserl did not call meanings *ideal* until 1894 (the 1894 essay on "Intentional Objects" may contain his first use of that adjective for meanings), his use of it in the very same year as Frege's review could hardly be an evidence of Frege's influence. While Husserl did consider Frege's review of his early work important (as Boyce Gibson's diary shows), its influence on him worked in ways other than has been generally taken to be the case. For this see chapter 2, part II. For *external* influences on Husserl, see references given in notes 54, 55, and 56 below. For the alleged psychologism of the *Philosophy der Arithmetik*, see references given in chapter 2, note 5.

46. E. Husserl, "Zur Logik des Zeichen," in *Philosophie der Arithmetik*, *Husserliana*, Vol. XII, pp. 340–373.

47. Ibid., pp. 303–348.

48. Ibid., pp. 349–356.

49. Husserl, *Logical Investigations*, II, Investigation V, Appendix to §§ 11 and 20.

50. E. Husserl, "Psychologische Studien zur elementaren Logik," *Philosophische Monatshefte*, 30 (1894):159–191, repr. in *Aufsätze und Rezensionen, Husserliana*, Vol. XXII, ed. B. Rang (The Hague: Martinus Nijhoff, 1979) pp. 92–123.

51. Husserl, *Logical Investigations*, I, p. 389.

52. Ibid., I, pp. 287–288.

53. Ibid., II, p. 688.

54. M. Farber writes, in my view justifiably, "If one reads all of Husserl's writings consecutively, one cannot but be impressed by the continuity of his development." Then Farber goes on to quote from a letter Husserl wrote to him: "External 'influences' are without significance . . . Really, my course was already marked out by the *Philosophie der Arithmetik*, and I could do nothing other than to proceed further" (M. Farber, *The Foundation of Phenomenology* (Cambridge, Mass.: Harvard University Press, 1943), p. 17.

55. For Lotze's influence on Frege, see H. Sluga, *Gottlob Frege* (London: Routledge & Kegan Paul, 1980).

56. E. Husserl, "Entwurf einer 'Vorrede' zu den 'Logischen Untersuchungen' (1913)," ed. E. Fink, *Tijdschrift voor Philosophie*, I (1939):106–133, 319–335.

57. Husserl's understanding of this Humean distinction was influenced by A. Reinach's "Kants Auffassung des Humeschen Problems," *Zeitschrift*

für Philosophie und philosophische Kritik, 141 (1908):176–209 ["Kant's Interpretation of Hume's Problem," trans. J.N. Mohanty, in *Southwestern Journal of Philosophy*, VII (1976):161–188].

58. Husserl, *Logical Investigations*, I, p. 179n.

59. Ibid., p. 292.

60. R. Aquila ("Husserl and Frege on Meaning," *Journal of the History of Philosophy* [1978]:373–383) and D. Willard ("The Paradox of Logical Psychologism: Husserl's Way Out," *American Philosophical Quarterly*, 9 [1972]:94–100, repr. in Mohanty, ed., *Readings on Edmund Husserl's "Logical Investigations"*) defend this earlier view of Husserl. Also cf. R. Bernet, "Bedeutung und intentionales Bewusstsein. Husserls Begriff des Bedeutungsphänomens," *Studien zur Sprachphänomenologie*, ed. E.W. Orth (Munich: Karl Alberg Verlag, 1979).

61. Cf. G. Küng, "The Phenomenological Reduction as Epoche and Explication," *The Monist*, 59 (1975):61–80; repr. in F. Elliston and P. McCormick, eds., *Husserl: Expositions and Appraisals* (Notre Dame, Ind.: University of Notre Dame Press, 1977).

62. Thus, Frege writes that logic has closer affinity with ethics: both are concerned with justification (*Posthumous Writings*, p. 4). Also: "Like ethics, logic can also be called a normative science" (Ibid., p. 128). While, not unlike Husserl, Frege adds that "these [normative] rules are prescribed by the laws of truth," so that logic is "the science of the most general laws of truth," he goes on to tell us that these laws of truth, like the principles of morals or the laws of the state, prescribe how we are to act (Ibid., p. 145). Although Frege may also be regarded as grounding the normativity of logic in a pure logic of truth, he does not suspect that a normative conception of logic may indeed be an ally of psychologism.

63. Cf., e.g., the introduction by M. Furth in G. Frege, *The Basic Laws of Arithmetic*, ed. and trans. M. Furth (Berkeley: University of California Press, 1964), esp. p. xviii.

64. Angelelli, *Studies on Gottlob Frege and Traditional Philosophy*, p. 53.

2. The Issue of Psychologism

1. From the *Begriffsschrift* (1879): "We can inquire, on the one hand, how we have gradually arrived at a given proposition and, on the other, how we can finally provide it with the most secure foundation. The first question may have to be answered differently for different persons; the second is more definite, and the answer to it is connected with the inner nature of the proposition considered" (Preface, G. Frege, *Frege's Conceptual Notation*, trans. T.W. Bynum [Oxford: Clarendon Press, 1972]). From the *Grundlagen* (1884): "Never let us take a description of the origin of an idea for a definition, or an account of the mental and physical conditions on which we become conscious of a proposition for a proof of it . . . a proposition no more ceases to be true when I cease to think of it than the sun ceases to exist when I shut my eyes" (G. Frege, *Foundations of Arithmetic*, 2nd rev. ed., trans. J.L. Austin [Evanston: Northwestern University Press, 1968] p. vi). From the *Grundgesetze* (1893): "Being true is different from being taken to be true, whether by one or many or everybody, and in no case is to be reduced to it. There is no contradiction in something's

being true which everybody takes to be false. I understand by 'laws of logic' not psychological laws of takings-to-be-true, but laws of truth . . . they are boundary stones set in an eternal foundation, which our thought can overflow, but never displace" (Introduction to the fourth edition, G. Frege, *The Basic Laws of Arithmetic*, ed. and trans. M. Furth [Berkeley: University of California Press, 1964], p. 13).

2. "Der Gedanke," in G. Frege, *Logische Untersuchungen*, ed. G. Patzig, (Göttingen: Vandenhoeck & Ruprecht, 1966), esp. pp. 30—31.

3. "Aufgabe und Bedeutung der 'Logische Untersuchungen,'" in E. Husserl, *Phänomenologische Psychologie, Husserliana*, Vol. IX., ed. W. Biemel (The Hague: Martinus Nijhoff, 1962), pp. 20—46. English translation, "The Task and Significance of the *Logical Investigations*," in J.N. Mohanty, ed., *Readings on Edmund Husserl's "Logical Investigations"* (The Hague: Martinus Nijhoff, 1977), p. 198. In *Formal and Transcendental Logic*, Husserl writes: "Nowhere in that volume was psychologism pure and simple (as a *universal* epistemological aberration) the theme. Rather, the discussion concerned *a psychologism with a quite particular sense*, namely the psychologizing of the irreal significational formations that are the theme of logic" (*Formal and Transcendental Logic*, trans. D. Cairns. [The Hague: Martinus Nijhoff, 1969], p. 152).

4. M. Sukale, *Comparative Studies in Phenomenology* (The Hague: Martinus Nijhoff, 1976), esp. ch. 1, "The Problem of Psychologism."

5. I agree with Hohlenstein's remark that "Husserl folgt keineswegs ahnungs- und problemlos der psychologistischen Tendenz der damals vorherrschenden philosophischen Strömung. Er vertritt einen wohl reflextierten, fest ungrenzten psychologischen Standpunkt." This position, according to Hohlenstein, coincides with that of Carl Stumpf, which seeks a mediation between psychologism and criticism (Introduction, E. Husserl, *Logische Untersuchungen*, Vol. I, *Prolegomena zur reinen Logik. Husserliana*, Vol. XVIII, ed. E. Hohlenstein [The Hague: Martinus Nijhoff, 1975], p. xix). Stumpf's "Psychologie und Erkenntnistheorie" was published in the same year in *Abhandlungen der philosophisch-philologische Klasse der königliche bayerischen Akademie der Wissenschaften*, 19 (1891):466—516.

6. Cf. T. De Boer, *The Development of Husserl's Thought*, trans. T. Plantinga (The Hague: Martinus Nijhoff, 1978), esp. pp. 116ff.

7. Cf. Hohlenstein's Introduction, *Husserliana*, Vol. XVIII, p. xxi.

8. E. Husserl, "Entwurf einer 'Vorrede' zu den 'Logischen Untersuchungen' (1913)," ed. E. Fink, in *Tijdschrift voor Philosophie*, I (1939):127.

9. E. Husserl, "Berichte über deutsche Schriften zur Logik aus dem Jahr, 1894," *Archiv für systematische Philosophie*, 3 (1897):226ff. (This review was written in 1897.)

10. E. Husserl, "Selbstanzeige," in *Vierteljahrsschrift für wissenschaftliche Philosophie*, 24 (1900):511—512.

11. J.N. Findlay, "Translator's Introduction," E. Husserl, *Logical Investigations*, trans, J.N. Findlay, Vol. I (New York: Humanties Press, 1970), p. 15.

12. Husserl, *Logical Investigations*, II, p. 782.

13. Ibid., pp. 782—784. Cf. De Boer, *Development of Husserl's Thought*, p. 120. De Boer insists that in the *Philosophie der Arithmetik* the correlation thesis is absent. Acts of a higher order have no correlative object.

Hence the need for reflection. Categorial objects as correlates of higher order acts first receive recognition in the *Logical Investigations*. Accordingly, for De Boer, the idea of constitution is also absent in the *Philosophie der Arithmetik*. It appears to me that the categorial objects are there in that early work, as correlates of appropriate acts.

14. E. Husserl, *Logical Investigations*, I, p. 373. For details of Husserl's theory of abstraction, see *Logical Investigations*, 2nd Inv., ch.3; M. Farber, *The Foundation of Phenomenology* (Cambridge, Mass.: Harvard University Press, 1943), ch. IX; J.N. Mohanty, *Edmund Husserl's Theory of Meaning*, *Phenomenologica*, Vol. 14, 3d ed. (The Hague: Martinus Nijhoff, 1976), pp. 25–28.

15. E. Husserl, *Ideas: General Introduction to Pure Phenomenology*, trans. W. Boyce Gibson (New York: Macmillan, 1931), ch. 1, § 13.

16. *Logical Investigations*, II, § 43.

17. E. Husserl, "Entwurf einer 'Vorrede' . . . ," p. 127.

18. For some of these objections, see "Husserl versus Frege, Selections from the *Philosophie der Arithmetik*," trans. E. Pivcevic, *Mind*, LXXVI (1967):155–165.

19. A. Church, "Review of M. Farber, *The Foundation of Phenomenology*," *Journal of Symbolic Logic*, 9 (1944):63–65.

20. W.R. Boyce Gibson, "From Husserl to Heidegger: Excerpts from a 1928 Freiburg Diary by W.R. Boyce Gibson," ed. H. Spiegelberg, *Journal of the British Society for Phenomenology*, 2 (1971):58–83.

21. A good example of the terminological care that must have been engendered by Frege's critique is to be found in the distinctions Husserl draws, in the *Logical Investigations*, between the various senses of the word *Vorstellung*. Earlier, in his *Grundlagen*, Frege had insisted that *Vorstellung* is understood either as subjective or as objective, and, in the objective sense, it may be taken either as object or as concept. Since this ambiguity had had undesirable consequences, Frege suggested that the word be used only in the subjective sense. Taken in this sense, the concept of *Vorstellung* should have no place in pure logic. Husserl, even in his strong anti-psychologistic phase, continues to speak of *Vorstellung* and to assign to it a central place in his logic. For this, see D. Føllesdal, *Husserl und Frege* (Oslo: Aschehoug, 1958), esp. pp. 32–33. But Husserl also proceeds to distinguish between many different senses in which the word is used (*Logical Investigations*, II, 5th Inv., ch. 6), from among which the strictly logical concept of *Vorstellung* is singled out: in this specifically logical sense, *Vorstellung* means either the meaning or the act in which the meaning is "realized."

22. Føllesdal, *Husserl und Frege*, esp. pp. 35–40.

23. J. Meiland, "Psychologism in Logic: Husserl's Critique," *Inquiry*, 19 (1976):325–339.

24. R.T. Nunn, "Psychologism, Functionalism, and the Modal Status of Logical Laws," *Inquiry*, 22 (1978):343–357.

25. *Logical Investigations*, I, ch. VII, § 36.

26. Ibid., p. 142.

27. G. Frege, "Logic," in *Posthumous Writings*, ed. H. Hermes, F. Kambartel, F. Kaulbach, trans. P. Long and R. White (Chicago: University of Chicago Press, 1979), pp. 126–151.

28. Ibid., p. 147.

29. Frege, "Der Gedanke," esp. pp. 48–49.

30. H. Sluga, *Gottlob Frege* (London: Routledge & Kegan, Paul, 1980), pp. 104–105.

31. *Posthumous Writings*, pp. 4, 128.

32. Frege, "Der Gedanke," p. 30.

33. Frege, *Basic Laws of Arithmetic*, p. 13.

34. Heidegger saw this clearly. The critique of psychologism, he pointed out in his 1925–26 logic lecture, is really a critique of a certain sort of psychology, and highlights the need for a new psychology through which phenomenology was to fulfill itself.

35. E. Husserl, "Selbstanzeige," pp. 511–512.

36. *Logical Investigations*, I, pp. 262–263.

37. See Hohlenstein, Introduction, in Husserl, *Logische Untersuchungen*, Vol. I, *Husserliana*, XVIII, p. xlvii.

38. *Logical Investigations*, I, p. 261.

39. Cf. R.M. Chisholm: "Brentano's descriptive psychology, though it appeals to experience and is therefore 'empirical' in Brentano's sense of the word, is not a psychology that only makes problematic induction from experience" ("Brentano's Descriptive Psychology," in *The Philosophy of Brentano*, ed. L.A. McAlister [Atlantic Heights, N.J.: Humanties Press, 1977], p. 98).

40. Husserl might have been thinking of this when he wrote that if one depends on the evidence of inner experience, particularly inner perception which *asserts existence*, then even if one speaks of 'apodictic evidence' and of 'a priori insights', one is still laboring under psychologism. "Phenomenological intuition . . . fundamentally excludes all psychological apperception and real (*reale*) assertion of existence . . ." (*Logical Investigations*, II, pp. 607–608).

41. For a stranger formulation of their difference, see T. De Boer, "The Descriptive Method of Franz Brentano: Its Two Functions and Their Significance for Phenomenology," in McAlister, ed., *Philosophy of Brentano*, pp. 101–107.

42. "One sees a thing, one has an idea, one apprehends, or thinks a thought" (G. Frege, "The Thought," trans. A. Quinton and M. Quinton, in *Essays on Frege* ed. E.D. Klemke [Urbana: University of Illinois Press, 1968]).

43. This is the view of Zocher, and, so it appears to me, of Sluga.

44. Frege, *Foundations of Arithmetic*, p. 36.

45. Angelelli and Sluga recognize this.

46. P.F. Linke, "Gottlob Frege als Philosoph," *Zeitschrift für philosophische Forschung*, 1 (1946–7):75–79.

47. See G. Bergmann, "Ontological Alternatives," in *Essays on Frege*, ed. Klemke, pp. 113–156, esp. pp. 128ff.

48. Ibid., p. 140.

49. Frege, *Posthumous Writings*, p. 145.

50. Ibid., p. 145.

51. *Logical Investigations*, I, p. 42.

52. P. Natorp. "On the Question of Logical Method," trans. J.N. Mohanty, in *Readings on Husserl's Logical Investigations*, ed. Mohanty, pp. 55–56, esp. p. 66.

53. Ibid., p. 66.

54. Earlier, in 1912, Heidegger had written: "G. Freges logisch-mathematische Forschungen sind meines Erachtens in ihrer wahren Be-

deutung noch nicht gewürdigt, geschweige denn ausgeschöpft. Was er in seinen Arbeiten 'Über Sinn und Bedeutung', 'Über Begriff und Gegenstand' niedergelegt hat, darf keine Philosophie der Mathematik übersehen; es ist aber auch in gleichen Masse wertvoll für eine allgemeine Theorie des Begriffs" (M. Heidegger, "Neuere Forschungen über Logik," *Gesamtausgabe*, Vol. 1: *Frühe Schriften*, ed. F.W. von Hermann [Frankfurt: Vittorio Klostermann, 1978], p. 20). It is interesting that Heidegger did not rate Bolzano equally highly. On the contrary, he writes that Husserl overrated Bolzano as a philosopher (*Gesamtausgabe*, Vol. 21: *Logik. Die Frage nach der Wahrheit*, ed. W. Biemel [Frankfurt: Vittorio Klostermann, 1976], p. 87.

55. *Gesamtausgabe*, Vol. 21, p. 92.

56. Ibid., p. 93.

57. To a similar objection by Palagyi that Husserl had created an "infinite abyss" between the two worlds, Husserl reponded in 1903: "Unfortunately, the author has read too selectively. Otherwise he would have stayed on guard against misinterpreting the *contrast* between ideal and real as *lack of relation* . . . as I have sufficiently explained, there can be derived from *any* ideal law whatsoever (e.g., any arithmetical law) universal truths about ideally possible or impossible connections of psychic fact" (E. Husserl, "A Reply to a Critic of My Refutation of Logical Psychologism," trans. D. Willard, *The Personalist* 53 (1972):5–13. Reprinted in *Readings on Husserl's Logical Investigations*, ed. Mohanty, esp. pp. 39–40.

58. E. Husserl, "Persönliche Aufzeichnungen," ed. W. Biemel, *Philosophy and Phenomenological Research*, XVI (1956):294.

59. Husserl, *Formal and Transcendental Logic*, esp. §§ 56, 57, 62, 64, 65, 67, and 99.

60. Ibid., p. 152.

61. Ibid., p. 172.

62. Cf.: "Nothing else hindered a clear insight into the sense, into the proper questions and methods, of genuine transcendental philosophy so much as did this anti-Platonism, which was so influential that it actuated all parties, and even thinking of a Kant, struggling to free himself from empiricism," Ibid., p. 259.

63. Ibid., § 99.

64. For more on this, see my "Consciousness and Lifeworld," *Social Research* (1975):147–166.

3. Theory of Sense

1. See especially E. Tugendhat, "The Meaning of 'Bedeutung' in Frege," *Analysis* 30 (June 1970):177–189.

2. G. Frege, *Posthumous Writings*, ed. H. Hermes, F. Kambartel, and F. Kaulbach, trans, P. Long and R. White (Chicago: University of Chicago Press, 1979), p. 99; idem, *The Basic Laws of Arithmetic*, ed. and trans, M. Furth (Berkeley: University of California Press, 1964), § 5, n.4.

3. G. Frege, *The Foundations of Arithmetic*, trans. J.L. Austin, 2d. rev. ed. (Evanston, Ill.: Northwestern University Press, 1968), p. 71.

4. *Posthumous Writings*, p. 187.

5. Ibid., p. 191.

6. Ibid.

7. Ibid., p. 192.

8. For the controversy about the context principle, see: H. Sluga, "Frege's Alleged Realism," *Inquiry*, 20 (1977):227–242; and M. Resnik, "Frege as Idealist and then Realist," *Inquiry*, 22 (1979):350–357.

9. M.A. Dummett, *Frege: Philosophy of Language* (New York: Harper & Row, 1973), p. 90.

10. Speaking provisionally, for truth and falsity for Frege are not real predicates.

11. Dummett, op.cit., p. 134.

12. E. Husserl, *Logical Investigations*, trans. J.N. Findlay, Vol. I (New York: Humanities Press, 1970), 1st Inv., § 12.

13. Curiously enough, Husserl takes 'one' to be a general name with extension. He should have said, using his own distinction, that it is a formal and not a general concept. Also, 'an equiliteral triangle' and 'an equiangular triangle' are misleadingly treated as names "whose indefiniteness gives them an extension." Frege rightly treats them as predicate expressions, having their own sense and reference though.

14. For more on this, see my "Husserl's Theory of Meaning," in *Husserl: Expositions and Appraisals*, ed. F. Elliston and P. McCormick (Notre Dame, Ind.: University of Notre Dame Press, 1977), pp. 18–35, esp. pp. 22–25.

15. See Appendix, Frege's letter to Husserl dated 24 May 1891, "Frege-Husserl Correspondence," trans. J.N. Mohanty, reprinted from *Southwestern Journal of Philosophy*, V (1974):83–95.

16. G. Frege, "On Schoenflies: Die Logischen Paradoxien der Mengenlehre," in *Posthumous Writings*, esp. p. 180.

17. Husserl writes: "Another view is, however, possible, which treats the *whole* state of affairs which corresponds to the statement as an analogue of the object a name names, and distinguishes this from the object's meaning" (*Logical Investigations*, I, p. 288). Dummett insists that in spite of Frege's misleading locutions it would be a mistake to treat truth values as being named by sentences. The relation between a sentence and its truth value is only analogous to that between a name and its bearer (Dummett, p. 183).

18. Husserl calls the sense or noema of judging 'proposition', e.g., in E. Husserl, *Formal and Transcendental Logic*, trans. D. Cairns (The Hague: Martinus Nijhoff, 1969).

19. G. Frege, *Logische Untersuchungen*, ed. G. Patzig (Göttingen: Vandenhoeck & Ruprecht, 1966), pp. 76. See also *Posthumous Writings*, p. 141.

20. "Frege-Husserl Correspondence," p. 191.

21. Frege has another, stricter criterion according to which if 'A believes S' is true and 'A believes S'' is not, then S and S' cannot have the same sense, i.e., cannot express the same thought. According to this intensional criterion, sentences provably or necessarily equivalent, may have different senses. The earlier criterion, as contrasted, is a purely logical and extensional one. Again, this is another of the tensions that persist in Frege.

22. "Meanings . . . constitute a class of 'universal objects' or species" (*Logical Investigations*, I, p. 331).

23. "Such change in meanings is really *change in the act of meaning*" (Ibid., p. 322).

24. "There is . . . no intrinsic connection between the ideal unities which in fact operate as meanings, and the signs to which they are tied"

(Ibid., p. 333). Husserl proceeds to say that there are unexpressed meanings.

25. Ibid., pp. 330, 323; II, p. 515.

26. *Formal and Transcendental Logic*, p. 134.

27. "Eine Tatsache ist ein Gedanke, der wahr ist" (from "Der Gedanke," Frege, *Logische Untersuchungen*, p. 50).

28. E. Husserl, *Formal and Transcendental Logic*, § 42.

29. E. Husserl, *Experience and Judgment*, trans. J. Churchill and K. Ameriks (Evanston, Ill.: Northwestern University Press, 1973), § 59, 60, 62, 65, 68, 69, 74, 78–79.

30. P. Geach and M. Black, eds., *Translations from the Philosophical Writings of Gottlob Frege* (Oxford: Basil Blackwell, 1952), p. 58.

31. Hans Sluga, *Gottlob Frege* (London: Routledge & Kegan Paul, 1980), esp. pp. 153–154.

32. Dummett, pp. 110ff., 227–232.

33. D. Bell, *Frege's Theory of Judgment* (Oxford: Clarendon Press, 1979).

34. Dummett, p. 227; Bell, p. 57. Bell allows 'elucidation' of sense, but not a precise specification of it.

35. Dummett, p. 110.

36. Bell, p. 76.

37. Dummett, p. 227.

38. Husserl, *Logical Investigations*, I, pp. 296–297, 430–431; II, pp. 495–498, 692–693, 774–775.

39. "In its relation to its object, the proper name is not an index." Ibid., p. 297.

40. E. Husserl, *Ideas: General Introduction to Pure Phenomenology*, Vol. I, trans. W.R. Boyce Gibson (New York: Macmillan, 1931). D. Welton has elaborated on this distinction in his various articles. See especially his "Structure and Genesis in Husserl's Phenomenology," in *Husserl: Expositions and Appraisals*, ed. F. Elliston and P. McCormick (Notre Dame, Ind.: Univ. of Notre Dame Press, 1977).

41. Husserl, *Logical Investigations*, I, p. 312.

42. Ibid., p. 315.

43. Ibid., pp. 315–316.

44. See especially T. Burge, "Sinning against Frege," *Philosophical Review*, LXXXVIII (1979):398–432.

45. The case with 'today' and 'yesterday' is just the reverse: their meanings are different, the referent and the senses may yet be the same.

46. According to Burge, with names we rely more on the person while with indexicals on context. In the case of 'I', however, the sense depends upon the speaker—not on what the speaker *intends* to mean, but on how the speaker thinks of himself. The sense therefore is determined by the speaker's beliefs and psychological state—beliefs about himself and psychological states through which he presents himself to himself. Cf. Burge, p. 423.

47. See J. Perry, "Frege on Demonstratives," *Philosophical Review*, LXXXVI (1977):474–497; idem, "The Problem of Essential Indexicals," *Nous*, XIII (1979):3–20.

48. Husserl, *Logical Investigations*, I, p. 315.

49. Ibid., II, 6th Inv., § 5.

50. Ibid., I, p. 315.

51. Frege, *Logische Untersuchungen*, p. 39; E.D. Klemke, ed., *Essays on Frege* (Urbana: University of Illinois Press, 1968), p. 519.

52. Husserl, *Logical Investigations*, I, p. 316.

53. *Formal and Transcendental Logic*, § 80.

54. Ibid., p. 199.

55. Frege, *Posthumous Writings*, p. 135. For further development of a theory of "essentially occasional expressions," making use of the idea of the horizontal structure of experience, see A. Gurwitsch, "Outlines of a Theory of 'Essentially Occasional' Expressions," in *Readings on Edmund Husserl's "Logical Investigations,"* ed. J.N. Mohanty (The Hague: Martinus Nijhoff, 1977), pp. 112–127.

56. Husserl, *Logical Investigations*, II, p. 675.

57. Ibid., I, p. 281.

58. Ibid., p. 277.

59. Ibid., II, p. 688.

60. Ibid.

61. For an account of the two theories, see literature listed in ch. 1, n. 60.

62. Burge, pp. 398–432.

63. M.A. Dummett, "Was Frege a Philosopher of Language?" *Revue Internationale de Philosophie* (1979):786–810, esp. pp. 805ff.

64. Ibid., p. 805.

65. Ibid., p. 808.

66. Ibid.

67. Husserl's phenomenological "description" of how a sense comes to be attached to a sign is in terms of the "fusion" of the act of uttering (the word or sentence) and the act of intending the sense. Whereas originally it is this fusion of acts that lends sense to an expressive act, it is a derivative consequence that the ideal contents of those acts—the word or sentence in itself and the sense—also enter into an inner unity, such that the expression is neither the mere word nor the mere sense, but their unity. Cf. *Logical Investigations*, I, pp. 280–282; II, pp. 582–583. The unity is so intimate that "we do not find in ourselves a mere sum of acts, but a single act in which, as it were, a bodily and a spiritual side are distinct" (Ibid., II, p. 583).

68. D. Føllesdal, "Husserl's Notion of Noema," *Journal of Philosophy*, 66 (1969):680–687.

69. A. Gurwitsch, *Studies in Phenomenology and Psychology* (Evanston, Ill.: Northwestern University Press, 1966), p. 337.

70. Ibid., p. 138.

71. Ibid., p. 341; Husserl, *Ideas*, I, p. 182.

72. Gurwitsch, *Studies in Phenomenology and Psychology*, p. 132.

73. Ibid., p. 134.

74. Ibid., p. 341.

75. Ibid., p. 440.

76. Cf. H. Drefus, "The Perceptual Noema: Gurwitsch's Crucial Contribution," in *Life-World and Consciousness: Essays for Aron Gurwitsch*, ed. L. Embree (Evanston, Ill.: Northwestern University Press, 1972), pp. 135–170, esp. p. 162.

77. Gurwitsch, *Studies in Phenomenology and Psychology*, p. 182.

78. Ibid., pp. 342, 347.

79. Ibid., p. 349.

80. Ibid.

81. Dreyfus, "The Perceptual Noema," esp. pp. 146–147.

82. Ibid., p. 147.

83. Husserl, *Logical Investigations*, II, p. 591.

84. Ibid., p. 591.

85. Ibid., p. 590.

86. Ibid., p. 738.

87. Ibid., p. 744.

88. Husserl, *Ideas*, I, p. 320.

89. Ibid., p. 324.

90. Ibid., p. 325.

91. Husserl, *Logical Investigations*, II, p. 670.

92. E. Husserl, *Analysen zur passiven Synthesis. Aus Vorlesungen- und Forschungsmanuskripten, 1918–1926*, ed. M. Fleischer, *Husserliana*, Vol. XI (The Hague: Martinus Nijhoff, 1966), p. 364.

93. For this way of putting it, I am indebted to M. Weinzweig's "On the Impossibility of Pure Description: Unphenomenological Aspects of Husserl's Phenomenology," Proceedings of Phenomenology Conference, 1976, Department of Philosophy, Australian National University, pp. 87–120.

94. A. Gurwitsch, *Studies in Phenomenology and Psychology*, pp. 138, 156–157.

95. A. Gurwitsch, *Phenomenology and the Theory of Science*, ed. L. Embree (Evanston, Ill.: Northwestern University Press, 1974).

96. Husserl, *Logical Investigations*, I, p. 289: "An expression only refers to an objective correlate *because* it means something, it can be rightly said to signify or name the object *through* its meaning."

97. Ibid., p. 329: "Such reflective talk really has as its object what serves as a meaning in straightforward talk." Also, p. 332: "If we perform the act and live in it, as it were, we naturally *refer* to its object and not to its meaning. . . . This latter first becomes objective to us in a reflex act of thought. . . ."

98. For different functions of the Fregean sense, see T. Burge, "Belief De Re," *Journal of Philosophy*, 74 (June 1977):338–361, and N. Salmon, "Review of Linsky, Names and Descriptions," *Philosophical Review* (1979):436–452.

99. H. Sluga emphasizes this: "Frege neither takes recourse to the notion of intuition when he talks about our knowledge of arithmetic, nor does he assume that seeing an object and grasping a thought are equivalent activities" (*Gottlob Frege*, p. 106).

100. Dreyfus favors this interpretation, as does John Searle. See Dreyfus's introduction in the volume of essays *Husserl, Intentionality and Cognitive Science*, ed. H. Dreyfus (Cambridge, Mass.: M.I.T. Press, forthcoming).

101. See especially J. Hintikka, *The Intentions of Intentionality* (Dordrecht: Reidel, 1975).

102. J.N. Mohanty, "Intentionality and Possible Worlds," in *Husserl, Intentionality and Cognitive Science*.

103. D. Føllesdal, "Husserl's Notion of Noema," esp. pp. 685–686.

104. Husserl, *Experience and Judgment*, p. 269.

105. Ibid.

106. Dummett, *Frege: Philosophy of Language*, p. 157.

107. Sluga, *Gottlob Frege*, pp. 60–61; 107.

108. J.N. Mohanty, "Husserl's Essentialism and Transcendental Phenomenology," *Review of Metaphysics*, XXXII (1978):229–321.

109. See Husserl, *Ideas*, I, ch. 1.

4. *Logic and Theory of Knowledge*

1. See "Frege against the Formalists (Excerpts from the *Grundgesetze der Arithmetik*)" in *Translations from the Philosophical Writings of Gottlob Frege*, ed. P. Geach and M. Black (Oxford: Basil Blackwell, 1952), pp. 162–213. Also see Frege's "Über formale Theorien der Arithmetik," repr. in *Freges kleine Schriften*, ed. I. Angelelli (Hildesheim: Georg Olms, 1967).

2. Geach and Black, p. 164.

3. Ibid., p. 166.

4. Ibid., p. 186.

5. Ibid., p. 207.

6. Ibid., pp. 212–213.

7. *Freges kleine Schriften*, p. 104.

8. W. Kneale and M. Kneale, *The Development of Logic* (Oxford: Clarendon Press, 1962), p. 510.

9. G. Frege, *Posthumous Writings*, trans. P. Long and R. White (Chicago: University of Chicago Press, 1979), p. 46.

10. Ibid., p. 12.

11. Ibid.

12. For the relation between the distinctions in the *Begriffsschrift* and the later works, see the Editor's Introduction in G. Frege, *Frege's Conceptual Notation*, trans. T.W. Bynum (Oxford: Clarendon Press, 1972), esp. p. 68.

13. See especially Frege, *Posthumous Writings*, p. 32.

14. E. Husserl, "Besprechung: E. Schröder, *Vorlesungen über die Algebra der Logik, I,*" *Göttingische gelehrte Anzeigen* (1891):258.

15. See Appendix, "Frege-Husserl Correspondence," trans. J.N. Mohanty, reprinted from *Southwestern Journal of Philosophy*, V (1974):83–95.

16. E. Husserl, "A. Voigts 'elementare Logik' und meine Darlegungen zur Logik des logischen Kalküls," *Vierteljahrsschrift für wissenschaftliche Philosophie*, 17 (1893):111–120, esp. p. 119.

17. G. Frege, "Excerpts from the Review of Schröder's Algebra," in *Translations from the Philosophical Writings of Gottlob Frege*, ed. P. Geach and M. Black (Oxford: Basil Blackwell, 1952), esp. p. 88.

18. Husserl, "Besprechung: E. Schröder . . . ," p. 247.

19. Husserl, "A. Voigts 'elementare Logik' . . . ," p. 119n.

20. E. Husserl, *Logical Investigations*, trans. J.N. Findlay, Vol. I (New York: Humanities Press, 1970), pp. 41–42.

21. Ibid., § 20.

22. Geach and Black, eds., p. 104.

23. Ibid., 106.

24. Frege, *Posthumous Writings*, p. 184. See also idem, *Philosophical and Mathematical Correspondence*, ed. G. Gabriel et al., trans. H. Kaal (Chicago: University of Chicago Press, 1980), p. 191 n. 69: "Accordingly, also the laws of classes are less primitive than those of concepts, and it is not suitable to found logic on the laws of classes." Also see p. 192, n. 71.

25. Frege, *Posthumous Writings*, p. 180.

26. M.A. Dummett, *Frege: Philosophy of Language* (New York: Harper & Row, 1973), p. 209.

27. M. Furth, Editor's Introduction, in G. Frege, *The Basic Laws of Arithmetic*, ed. and trans. M. Furth (Berkeley: University of California Press, 1964), pp. xxxix–xlii.

28. Ibid., p. xliii.

29. H. Sluga, *Gottlob Frege* (London: Routledge & Kegan Paul, 1980), pp. 146–148.

30. Frege, *Posthumous Writings*, p. 183.

31. Frege, *Phiolosophical and Mathematical Correspondence*, p. 192, n. 71.

32. Frege, *Posthumous Writings*, p. 122.

33. The same is true of concepts: "Even if we concede to the intensionalist logicians that it is the concept as opposed to the extension that is the fundamental thing, this does not mean that it is to be taken as the sense of a concept word: it is its reference, and the extensionalist logicians come closer to the truth insofar as they are presenting—in the extension—a *reference* as the essential thing" (Ibid., p. 123).

34. Ibid., p. 128.

35. Ibid., p. 3.

36. E. Husserl, "Der Folgerungskalkül und die Inhaltslogik," *Vierteljahrsschrift für wissenschaftliche Philosophie*, 15 (1891):168–189, 351–356.

37. For a critical evaluation of this claim, see Gilbert Null's review of Husserl's *Aufsätze und Rezensionen*, *Southwestern Journal of Philosophy*, XI, no. 3 (1980):155–164.

38. Husserl, *Logical Investigations*, I, pp. 322–323.

39. E. Husserl, *Formal and Transcendental Logic*, trans. D. Cairns (The Hague: Martinus Nijhoff, 1969), p. 137.

40. Husserl, *Logical Investigations*, II, pp. 456–458.

41. Ibid., p. 827.

42. Husserl, *Formal and Transcendental Logic*, part I, ch. 3.

43. Ibid., § 31, p. 96.

44. Frege's conditional is truth-functional, the implication is material implication. Husserl's implication is some form of strict implication.

45. Frege, *Posthumous Writings*, p. 175. Contrast Husserl: to say that logic is concerned with judgments, affirmations, denial, inference, etc., would be psychologism (*Logical Investigations*, I., pp. 323–324).

46. Frege, *Philosophical and Mathematical Correspondence*, p. 182.

47. Cf. Dummett, p. 309.

48. Thiel sees this point. See his *Sense and Reference in Frege's Logic* (Dordrecht: Reidel, 1968), p. 105. Dummett (pp. 312–313, 362) dispels this anxiety by construing assertion as a conventional social act.

49. Husserl, *Formal and Transcendental Logic*, § 45. See also §§ 44, 48, 49.

50. Sluga, p. 115.

51. Contrast the following sentence from a Frege manuscript (of 1906 or earlier): "The task of logic is to set up laws according to which a judgment is justified by others, irrespective of whether these are themselves true" (*Posthumous Writings*, p. 175. Italics mine).

52. For this, see D. Bell, *Frege's Theory of Judgment* (Oxford: Clarendon Press, 1979), pp. 120–121.

53. Cf. O. Kraus, *Franz Brentano: Mit Beiträgen von Carl Stumpf und Edmund Husserl* (Munich: C.H. Beck, 1919), esp. pp. 106–107.

54. Brentano also held the view that an entire class of judgments, called by him *indirect* judgments (such as, "It is possible, probable, necessary, true, false, that . . ."), relate to such contents. Stumpf notes that later in his life Brentano changed this view about indirect judgments and came to hold that all judgments related to the *real* (Ibid., p. 133).

55. For Kant's theory of judgment, see L.W. Beck, *Studies in the Philosophy of Kant* (Indianapolis: Bobbs-Merrill, 1965), ch. 4.

56. See Frege, *Posthumous Writings*, pp. 2, 139.

57. "One can say that to make a judgment is to make a choice between opposites. Rejecting the one and accepting the other is one and the same act" (Ibid., p. 187).

58. Ibid., p. 177.

59. Ibid., p. 178.

60. Cf. I. Kant, *Critique of Pure Reason*, trans. N.K. Smith (London: Macmillan, 1933), p. 106.

61. The thesis perhaps is directly taken from Lotze who construed the Platonic Ideas to be propositional rather than concepts. Only propositions, Lotze held, have *Geltung*.

62. On this last point, cf. Sluga, pp. 90–93.

63. E. Husserl, "Bericht über deutsche Schriften zur Logik 1895–1898," *Archiv für systematische Philosophie*, 9 (1903), esp. pp. 237–238.

64. Ibid., pp. 243–245.

65. Husserl, *Formal and Transcendental Logic*, p. 134.

66. Husserl's analysis of judgment into (a) an act of positing the subject, (b) an act of positing a predicate, (c) an act of attribution or denial, and, then, finally (d) an overriding act of belief, corresponds closely to John Searle's distinctions between the act of referring, the act of predicating, and the illocutionary acts.

67. Husserl, *Formal and Transcendental Logic*, pp. 121, 196.

68. Husserl, *Logical Investigations*, II, 5th Inv., § 28 footnote.

69. Ibid., pp. 612–613.

70. For this distinction, see E. Husserl, *Experience and Judgment*, trans. J. Churchill and K. Ameriks (Evanston, Ill.: Northwestern Univ. Press, 1973), §§ 71–72.

71. For discussion of "assent" and "acceptance," see Husserl, *Logical Investigations*, II, pp. 613–616.

72. Husserl, *Experience and Judgment*, pp. 288–289.

73. Ibid., p. 293.

74. For an account of Husserl's theory of dependent and independent meanings, see J.N. Mohanty, *Edmund Husserl's Theory of Meaning*, 3d ed. (The Hague: Martinus Nijhoff, 1976), pp. 86–93. For the present purpose, it is important to note that as a consequence of (i) his distinction between the founding-funded and part-whole relations, and (ii) the thesis that judging is a constituting, synthetic form*ing* act, Husserl did not accept the rigid one-to-one correspondence that Fregean *semantics* appears to have posited between (1) the parts of a sentence, (2) the parts of the thought that the sentence expresses, and (3) the referents of the component sentence parts. Here phenomenology departs from semantics.

75. Husserl, *Logical Investigations*, II, p. 632.

76. Husserl, *Formal and Transcendental Logic*, pp. 209–300.

77. Husserl, *Logical Investigations*, I, p. 431.

78. Husserl, *Formal and Transcendental Logic*, p. 295.

79. Ibid., pp. 295–96.

80. In E. Husserl, *Idea of Phenomenology*, trans. W.P. Alston and G. Nakhnikian (The Hague: Martinus Nijhoff, 1964).

81. Cf. P. Kitcher, "Frege's Epistemology," *Philosophical Review*, LXXXXVIII (1979):235–262.

82. Cf. G. Prauss, "Freges Beitrag zur Erkenntnistheorie," *Allgemeine Zeitschrift für Philosophie*, 1, no. 1 (1976):34–61.

83. Frege, *Posthumous Writings*, p. 267.

84. Prauss (op. cit.) draws attention to these striking texts and their idealistic implications.

85. G. Frege, "The Thought," trans. A. Quinton and M. Quinton, repr. in E. Klemke, ed., *Essays on Frege* (Urbana: University of Illinois Press, 1968), esp. p. 529.

86. Ibid., p. 532.

87. Immediately after the passage quoted above, Frege continues, "So since the answer lies in the *non-sensible,* perhaps *something non-sensible* could also lead us out of the inner world and enable us to grasp thoughts where no sense impressions were involved. . . . We should need something non-sensible for the recognition of both realms [i.e., outer, sensible world and thoughts]. . . . Recognition of thoughts leads us from the inner to the external world. What makes it possible to apprehend the thoughts themselves? Prauss (p. 51) finds in the locution "something non-sensible" suggestions for the Kantian doctrine of "transcendental object" as the spontaneous and original projection of a non-sensible object through which it is first of all possible to have something like an external object at all. I detect a much closer affinity with Husserl's concept of *noema.*

88. Frege, *Posthumous Writings*, p. 3.

89. Frege, *Philosophical and Mathematical Correspondence*, p. 164.

90. G. Frege, "Über Sinn und Bedeutung," *Zeitschrift für Philosophie und philosophische Kritik*, n.f., 100 (1892):25–50; rep. in Frege, *Funktion, Begriff und Bedeutung*, ed. G. Patzig (Göttingen: Vandenhoek & Ruprecht, 1962), in which see esp. p. 48.

91. This manuscript is included in Frege, *Posthumous Writings*.

5. *Conclusion*

1. Among Frege commentators, Bell sees this contrast clearly, even if not in its full depth and potentiality: D. Bell, *Frege's Theory of Judgment* (Oxford: Clarendon Press, 1979), pp. 78ff.

2. For a contrast between naturalistic and transcendental understandings of intentionality, see my "Intentionality and Noema," *Journal of Philosophy*, LXXVIII (November 1981):706–717.

3. For the role of the perceptual paradigm in *de re* relief, see T. Burge, "Belief De Re," *Journal of Philosophy*, LXXIV (June 1977):338–362. For further on *de re* intentionality and perceptual noema, see Mohanty, op. cit., § IV, and also "Husserlian Phenomenology and the *de re* and *de dicto* Intentionalities," forthcoming in *Researches in Phenomenology*.

INDEX

147